When OCD symptoms beg
can be profoundly confusi
who don't understand OCD often offer advice that is not only unhelpful, but can actually make matters worse. Mike Kheir clearly understands this struggle. In this refreshingly honest and vulnerable book, Mike shares his personal journey of struggling with OCD as a Christian. He has done his homework, and he shares how understanding OCD as a medical disorder is not incompatible with true faith in Christ. This is a much-needed resource for Christians who have been tormented with OCD attacking their faith. In these pages, you will find one man's honest story, valuable and solid information, and hope.

—**Mark E. Crawford,** Ph.D.

Dr. Crawford is the author of *The Obsessive-Compulsive Trap: Real Help for a Real Disorder.* He is the former team psychologist for the Atlanta Hawks of the NBA; has appeared on ABC's Good Morning America, ABC's World News This Morning, House Call with Dr. Sanjay Gupta, and has made multiple appearances on CNN and CNN Headline News.

Michael Kheir provides us with a fascinating account of his long journey through a difficult case of childhood onset OCD. Well written and poignant, Kheir describes in vivid detail a host of religiously-themed obsessional fears that caused him torment. Kheir also catalogues and details the use of the cognitive and faith-based strategies that have worked best to overcome his terrors. There is something in this book for every Christian OCD sufferer.

—**Ian Osborn**, MD

Dr. Osborn is a Christian, a psychiatrist, a former professor at Penn State University & The University of New Mexico, and an OCD sufferer. He is author of the books *Tormenting Thoughts and Secret Rituals: The Hidden Epidemic of Obsessive-Compulsive Disorder* and *Can Christianity Cure Obsessive-Compulsive Disorder? A Psychiatrist Explores the Role of Faith in Treatment.*

WAGING WAR AGAINST OCD

A CHRISTIAN APPROACH TO VICTORY

MICHAEL KHEIR

LUCIDBOOKS

Waging War Against OCD
A Christian Approach to Victory

Published by Lucid Books in Houston, TX
www.LucidBooks.com

ISBN: 978-1-63296-617-9 (paperback)
eISBN: 978-1-63296-618-6

Special Sales: Most Lucid Books titles are available in special quantity discounts. Custom imprinting or excerpting can also be done to fit special needs. Contact Lucid Books at Info@LucidBooks.com

For you did not receive the spirit of bondage again to fear, but you received the Spirit of adoption by whom we cry out, "Abba, Father." The Spirit Himself bears witness with our spirit that we are children of God.

Romans 8:15–16

For we do not have a High Priest who cannot sympathize with our weaknesses, but was in all points tempted as we are, yet without sin. Let us therefore come boldly to the throne of grace, that we may obtain mercy and find grace to help in time of need.

Hebrews 4:15–16

And you shall know the truth, and the truth shall make you free.

John 8:32

To Rash

Who shows grace, acceptance, and forgiveness when I allow my OCD to turn on her in the ugliest of ways. For believing in this book more than I did and allowing me to take a year off work to write the foundation of this book. For performing extended edits to get the manuscript to the finish line.

To Gedo

For his patience, perseverance, and Christlike boldness. For his example of strong faith and his diligence in answering all my questions about the Bible.

To Ann M. Eng

For taking so much time to organize, edit, and greatly improve the original version of this book. God truly used you to make this book become a reality.

SPECIAL THANKS

Mom

I am sure my OCD was a burden on you when I was a child and even into my early 20s, so thank you for always being there for me throughout my life, and for your constant love and encouragement.

Dawn

Thank you for your genuine interest in the manuscript, and your desire to see this get to the finish line. Your introduction to Charlie truly lifted me up and really motivated me to finish. Your endless encouragement, texts asking about the book's status, and your willingness to always talk through the different stages encouraged me more than you know.

Michelle S

Thank you for taking time out of your busy life to teach the writing workshop at Venture Christian Church in 2015. Without your coaching and mentoring, the Prologue and much of Chapter 2 would have never been written.

TABLE OF CONTENTS

PROLOGUE

RACHEL'S HORROR STORY

Rachel is a project manager in her early thirties. She graduated with honors from a top university and has a decent job. Today starts a little more tense than most, but it is bearably hectic. Although the walk from her car to the entrance of her air-conditioned office is only 30 yards, she is sweating from the brutal Texas summer heat. It's already 88 degrees, and it's only 8:12 a.m. She thinks to herself: "*What a stressful morning that was! And only 12 minutes late, not too bad.*" She knows the importance of salvaging her reputation at work. She's been chronically late or has simply gone missing for 45 minutes to an hour a couple times a month since she started eight months ago. Her work ethic is strong, and she has shown her boss that she can outperform her peers. Her innovation makes her a valuable asset, but being unreliable is something she knows won't be tolerated forever.

Removing her laptop from its bag, she hooks it up to the docking station and turns it on. As she heads to the lunchroom for her first cup of coffee, she bumps into Tim, a coworker and friend for the past 15 years. He helped her land the job almost a year ago.

"You ready for the meeting?" he asks kindly.

"Yep, I went over all the data again last night. I could probably present without even looking at the slides," she responds with an air of confidence.

Tim also notices a touch of *leave me the heck alone* in her tone and assumes she is more nervous about the presentation than she wants to let on. He concludes that she doesn't want to talk about it until it's over. "Good to hear, and don't miss this one," he says half-jokingly, referring to a meeting she had inexplicably missed a couple months before. Rachel tries to shrug the conversation off, but she can't shake the anxiety caused by the magnitude of the meeting.

As she heads back to her desk, a thought strikes her violently, filling her with panic, almost causing her to drop to the floor. Her body begins to tremor; maintaining her composure just to get back to her chair seems impossible and takes all the strength she can muster. She barely makes it back and sits down, while her mind races with visions of her infant son flailing helplessly. Rachel had taken the baby to their enclosed patio while she scarfed down her breakfast just 25 minutes ago. She had only spent a few minutes there because the patio gets unbearably hot in the summers, even by eight o'clock in the morning. But she often eats breakfast there in hopes of seeing deer walking along the path below—something she and her neighbor often discuss. The patio is furnished but under construction, and the contractors cautioned them to use it carefully as there are still areas of flooring that need work.

"It must be 130 degrees in that room by now!" she thinks to herself. Images of her 14-month-old son, Gabriel, torture her. *"He could be dead by now,"* she thinks and begins to imagine how it could have ended. *"Did he suffer? Did he suffocate?"* She can't bear the thought of his last moments, as the panic and screaming probably turned to lighter and shorter breaths . . . and finally, eerie

silence. She begins fixating on the painful thoughts of never seeing him again, being viewed as a monster, or being held criminally negligent, at best. Her blood pressure rises, and she clenches her forehead with both hands in an attempt to erase the images from her mind. She finally lets out a big sigh.

"Everything OK?" asks Jen, who sits in the communal cube next to her.

"I'm fine," Rachel replies even though she knows she is anything but. She grabs her office phone to call her husband but knows that's not an option. She could never muster the courage to tell him what she had to say. Her heart is racing; what was slight perspiration has turned to a bath underneath her shirt. She starts an internal monologue: "*My meeting starts in just 20 minutes; there is no way I can go to that meeting now. How dare I even think of going to the meeting! Do I have no soul? What mother would be sitting here in this situation? But the odds of saving him are so minuscule . . . . There's no time to consider that, I have to run home immediately! Is it worth risking my livelihood over this? What type of mother would even be thinking like this? I need to leave now! It could be the difference between the life and death of my only son!*"

Despite her raging thoughts, she tries to calm her mind enough to think through the situation. Looking up at her computer, she notices a new email. It's from her boss. Something came up, and he had to reschedule the meeting for later in the week. She begins to persuade herself that this must be a sign from God! The ritualistic prayers begin, and she finally grabs her keys and starts toward the exit. The flurry of thoughts causes her to bump into Matt who works on the shop floor. He had turned her in a few months ago for leaving work midday without letting her boss know. It was just a slight ding on her reputation, and she and Matt smoothed things over since then and were on good speaking terms, but she couldn't possibly let him see her leave.

"Hey, watch it!" he says playfully.

"How can this be happening? I have to go now!" The thoughts race through her mind. Playing it cool, she says, "My bad," in an equally lighthearted way. Instead of heading for the exit, she turns into the bathroom. She hides in a stall and tries to gather her thoughts. Despite her attempts to stop shaking, remaining there only intensifies her panic.

"Every moment counts," she whispers to herself. She leaves the bathroom and heads for the exit, noticing that Matt isn't in the hallway anymore. "Thank you, God," she prays, her walk turning to a run as she heads to her car and starts the engine. She looks down at the clock and sees that it's 8:19 a.m. It's only been seven minutes since she parked her car, but it feels like hours. As she gets about a half mile down the road, she begins to relax.

"I'm doing all I can do; it's the right thing to do. How could I not go back home? I'm not a monster. God tells us to love one another. How unloving would it be to not see if I can save my child?" She turns on the radio, hoping to distract herself from the situation she finds herself in. She gently begins singing along to a few words of the song on the radio, momentarily forgetting the nightmare that the morning has turned into.

As she pulls into her driveway, the terrifying thoughts return. "Finally, home!" she screams as she flings her car door open. Running from the car, she fumbles for her house key. As she makes her way to the foot of the stairs, she hears, "Forgot your laptop again?" in a teasing tone. She swings around and sees her neighbor, Anne, a stay-at-home mom, on her way to the park with her toddlers.

Rachel looks down at Anne's older son and smiles. He's distracted by something on the ground and doesn't even notice her. She looks back up at Anne who gives her a puzzled look. Rachel can't even muster a response; she's too embarrassed. She runs up the steps, unlocks the front door, and sprints to the enclosed patio.

She opens the door and scans the room. It's dead silent and unbearably hot. Her heart pounds even faster: facing what's next will be grueling. She looks at the corner where Gabriel was placed an hour before. She walks to each of the four corners of the room and looks at the opposite side. No angle can be missed. Her search must be done perfectly, or it's all for naught. There must be complete certainty that her son is not in the room.

She frantically pulls the throw pillows off the couch and recliner, followed by the seat cushions—still no sign of Gabriel. Yet, there is no rest; he could be under something. She gets down on the floor and looks under the couch, recliner, and coffee table. She heads toward the grandfather clock. If she contorts her shoulders just the right way, she can squeeze enough of her face between the clock and wall so that one of her eyes can make out if anything is there. The odds of a baby being there are essentially zero, but that makes no difference. The checking must be done with precision . . . doing all she can to save her child is her only focus.

The area rug is thick, far too heavy for her to pick up on her own. She begins pulling up the corners and doesn't see anything underneath. She stops for a minute to catch her breath, and soaks in some of the insanity that has become her life.

"Might as well finish what I started." The thought passes through her mind, a sentiment both sadistic and sarcastic. Frantically, she moves all the furniture close to the walls so that it no longer pins the rug to the floor. She rolls the entire rug to one side. She knows there's always a one in a billion chance he's stuck under the one spot the rug is rolled on. So she unrolls it and rolls up the opposite side to make sure she can see under there. After all, there could be a hole in the floor trapping her son under the rug: she has to check every single inch of the room, or she'll have to start over.

As she leans their six-foot plant to one side, she bends over as far as she can to make sure nothing is between the base of the planter and the floor. It really is 130 degrees in the room, and sweat drips off her as if she's standing in a steady rain. Ironically, she puts her hands on her hips and begins to laugh at herself. Nothing is funny about this, and her laughter turns to tears and then to laughter again. As the sweat and tears stream off her nose, she realizes that she is dehydrated and her vision is beginning to blur. She can't continue the search.

She walks to the kitchen and pours a glass of water. Light-headed, she heads to the TV room and sits on the floor. After a few moments of catching her breath, the dread and panic return. "Wait, did I check behind the right side of the grandfather clock?" She puts down her glass and heads for the patio that she is growing to loathe the sight of. She begins contorting so she can see through the one-inch gap between the wall and clock. "Wait, was this the side I was sure I checked?" she asks herself, before going to the other side to check again just to be extra sure.

Rachel begins to doubt where she has looked, so she spends another few minutes rechecking all the same places. Finally, her anxiety lessens now that she is certain her son is not there. She heads back to the TV room, opens the coffee-table drawer, pulls out her journal and starts flipping through the pages as she counts, "8, 9 . . . 12 . . . 15, 16 . . . and now 17," she says in defeat. Seventeen times she had turned around or left work in the last eight months, having done this exact same thing. Rachel begins documenting today's episode because she has found that doing so soothes her after episodes like this.

The process hadn't always been so in-depth. When this first started, she would just look in the room from the outside, see that it was empty and then head straight back to her car. "Well at least I got all the way to work this time," she says laughing to herself: most times she would turn around before she had driven a mile from home.

The thoughts of her son suffocating in that room are gone. Despite all her emotions and every fiber of her being screaming otherwise, somewhere deep down, she had known that her husband had left with Gabriel and taken him to daycare just minutes after she left the house. Today was not her day to drop him off. Temporary relief is slowly being replaced by the worries of reality. However, new thoughts begin racing through her mind about the impact that episodes like this have on work and her family. Her husband Jim certainly struggles with this behavior.

"Jim will be furious when he hears about this. Anne will only cover for me so many times," she thinks. *If Matt finds out that I pulled this again, he'll surely mention it to my boss. The last thing I need right now is another ding on my record.* She promises herself this will never happen again, but she's starting not to believe that when she says it. Thoughts of how to stop the destructive patterns don't cross her mind. They never have. Most of her energy now centers on getting through the day, not getting fired, providing for her family, and just getting by.

She rushes back to her car to head back to work, glancing at a picture she's had on her dashboard for years. It's a photo of Rachel with her parents at her college graduation. Although she looks almost the same, she sees the carefree and self-confident girl in the photo as somebody else. As she backs out of the driveway, dark and familiar thoughts pass through her mind: "*What is wrong with me? Am I crazy? No one will ever understand me. I can't let anyone know about this.*" This is bigger than just her weak will, and she doesn't know how to shake it. These episodes have left her feeling hopeless and constantly exhausted. She's starting to isolate, and this issue has created a mountain between her and her husband, family, friends, and coworkers. She's in desperate need of answers to her questions. She rejects all the negative thoughts and emotions, clinging to the only thing she knows anymore—that the promises of God are true and that heaven won't include this madness. Little does she know, she has a disorder that plagues millions of people. She has OCD.

PART I:

BEGINNINGS AND QUESTIONS

CHAPTER 1
INTRODUCTION

Approximately 2.5% of the US population is diagnosed with OCD[1] which, at the time of this writing, is about 8.3 million people. Therefore, at least a small portion of the 8.3 million people with OCD are Christians fighting the same battle day in and day out. This is proof by the numbers that we are not alone in our struggle. However, many of us struggle in isolation.

Now in my 40s, I have struggled with OCD since I was a child. I've experienced much pain in my efforts to combat this illness, and I've sought many different avenues for healing that addressed the mental, physical, and spiritual aspects of health. As a Christian with OCD, I tried to please God and understand Him. All the while, I struggled with self-condemnation and a distorted understanding of God's character and what it means to have a genuine faith. As others with OCD may understand, I also struggled with a lack of understanding from those who tried to help me and who loved and cared for me. I credit a combination of medicine, counseling, Christian fellowship, and a corrected understanding of biblical truth with helping me fight this disorder. But most of all, I credit God himself, the work of Christ on the cross, and the power of the Holy Spirit for giving me the most victory. I can now say that with God's grace and help, I can overcome OCD. I'm not 100% cured, but I have overcome crippling OCD and have learned how to practice victory over it. And thus, I offer this book.

What Is OCD?

OCD is a diagnosable medical condition—a mental disorder marked by excessive fear or anxiety, which becomes an obsession. A person's intense focus and fixation on the fear leads to compulsions. Compulsions are behaviors that OCD sufferers perform in a desperate attempt to control or relieve the fear and anxiety. People who have OCD exhibit differences in brain chemistry versus people who do not. The following demonstrates the cycle of OCD:

- Obsessions (intrusive thoughts) produce anxiety.
- Anxiety produces compulsions meant to reduce anxiety.
- Compulsions bring temporary relief.
- Temporary relief ends and is replaced by more obsession.
- The cycle gains strength as it is repeated.

Practically speaking, here is what the cycle looks like:

1. Fear and anxiety (e.g., "My parents might get into a car accident on their way to work.")
2. False beliefs (e.g., "I should have been nicer to my parents this morning because maybe they would have decided to stay home with me and thus would avoid potentially being killed in a car accident.")
3. False burdens of responsibility (e.g., "The way I talk to my parents before they leave for work will determine whether they go to work and thus get into a car accident. I am responsible for preventing them from having a car accident.")

4. Ineffective methods of relieving the original fear, which become relentless (e.g., "If I had more joy in the Lord, I would have been nicer to my parents; therefore, I should read my Bible longer each morning.")
5. A false sense of control and a tendency to increase compulsions to gain a greater sense of control (e.g., "I will read the Bible for 30 minutes each morning; therefore, my parents won't get into a car accident. I must do this perfectly, without bad thoughts or interruption.")

As you can see from these examples, OCD not only impacts the emotional life and daily functioning of the person with the disorder, but for those who have faith in God through Christ, the illness also affects our understanding of God and how we are to live out our faith. If the child in the examples above used to love reading his Bible, would he now be doing so out of desire to know God more fully? Or would it become a legalistic chore as he began to believe that reading his Bible was a way to prevent his parents from being hurt? If he can't maintain his strict standards for reading the Bible, does he become trapped in paralyzing repetition to try to get it right? And if he can't get it "right," does he carry the torment of misplaced guilt? Does this strategy for preventing danger reflect how God wants him to simply rest and trust?

Why This Book?

I remember sitting in a Christian therapist's office when I was 28. He was the third professional I had met with to discuss my disorder. He made a joke about OCD and then paused before saying something no one had ever said to me before: "I know this is your torment. I don't have OCD, but I have helped numerous people with your condition and have seen the anguish they go through." The most convincing thing about his words was the way he said them. He had a genuine sadness in his eyes, which made me realize he might actually understand the enormity of my struggle—the unending and vicious thought patterns, the merciless and time-consuming behavioral regimens, the constant guilt, the frustration of knowing that no one around me understood my burden, and the fear of being publicly humiliated.

At that point in my life, I had experienced enough victory in managing my OCD that I was able to be comforted by his words without becoming overly dependent on him. But I couldn't help feeling sad. Where was that much-needed understanding from someone who could have helped me when I was a child consumed by condemnation, confusion, and destructive behaviors? Or when I was a teenager and young adult, living a life wracked with torment?

As the year with this empathetic therapist progressed, I found myself investigating more about OCD. After searching the internet for ways to cope with OCD as a Christian, I realized most books on the subject focused solely on medical analyses and diagnoses. Where was the practical help for me? Where was the comfort of knowing that a community of Christians understood my struggle and had identified wise and practical approaches to combating it? I found only one such community—a Christian OCD support group at Willow Creek Community Church in Chicago, which has unfortunately disbanded at the time of the writing of this book.

I wanted to write a book for all Christians affected by OCD and for those who know and love them. It is also my hope that pastors and Christian counselors, psychiatrists, and psychologists will read this book and gain greater insight into the mind of a Christian OCD sufferer. I've had well-meaning Christians tell me to focus on my problems as if they were solely spiritual, and I've had a non-Christian psychiatrist tell me to just take medication (and stop reading my Bible!). As I continued my research, I was surprised to learn that several respected and effective therapeutic approaches with scientific and brain-based foundations align with truths found in Scripture.

I concluded that because this illness affects every aspect of the person (including the physical brain, mind, and soul), a more integrated approach multiplies the benefits not achievable by one approach alone. It is my hope that this book will be used to:

- Bring new insight into how the Word of God can be used as a powerful tool in the treatment of OCD.
- Encourage mental health professionals to show their Christian clients and patients that scientifically proven methods of therapy align with Scripture.
- Lend insight into the physical and emotional aspects of OCD that church leaders, lay counselors, and the larger church community may not understand. In my experience, many Christians lack awareness of OCD. This book aims to change that and to increase awareness of how to help someone with OCD fight the Christian fight of faith.
- Underscore that taking medication does not reflect a lack of faith. I found that medication can be very effective at soothing obsessions and compulsions and may provide OCD sufferers with the rest and mental space they need to gather arms to battle this disorder. Nonetheless, I do not believe that medication alone can replace what I have received from knowing God.
- Reveal how we, by faith, can use the power of the Holy Spirit in us, the Word of God, and fellowship with other believers to experience victory over OCD.

My ability to write this book demonstrates God's amazing faithfulness, grace, and provision in my life. I hope it will convince every reader that God is faithful to keep us until the day of redemption. I refer not only to the truth of eternal salvation, but to the truth of daily sanctification—growing more in His image.

A Message for Those with OCD

You are not alone. I understand what it's like to genuinely try to do the right thing and hit dead end after dead end . . . what it's like to reach out for help and get confusing advice and mixed or even condemning responses . . . what it's like to diligently seek God and hold closely to the promise that Christ is sufficient . . . what it's like to believe that you will never find the answer to this disease . . . and what it's like not knowing how to reconcile the biblical promises of a victorious and joyful life with the continuous defeat you experience as a result of anxious and ritualistic thoughts.

Sometimes, OCD has been so overwhelming that forming a single logical thought seemed nearly impossible. The only thing that kept me going in those moments was the fact that I knew God was good and that He was faithful to me. I remember when crying out to God seemed impossible because I thought I was so outside God's will that my prayers would only be a slap in His face. Despite those false beliefs and overwhelming emotions, I focused on remembering what it was like when I *could* fully enjoy being in His presence. Those reflections gave me the will and strength to believe that I could overcome OCD by God's grace.

Always remember that God's love for you is inescapable. "God loves you, and you have no say in the matter." This truth is a quote from Christian comedian and singer Mark Lowry, who struggled with ADHD as a child and felt like he might never amount to anything. No matter how condemned we feel by OCD, how much we give in to our compulsions, or how much we think we have done to damage ourselves and our relationship with God and others, it is comforting to know we can't do anything about what

God thinks about us. He loves us unconditionally, wants us to feel loved, and wants us to respond to that love.

> *Love is patient, love is kind. It does not envy, it does not boast, it is not proud. It does not dishonor others, it is not self-seeking, it is not easily angered, it keeps no record of wrongs. Love does not delight in evil but rejoices with the truth. It always protects, always trusts, always hopes, always perseveres. Love never fails.*
>
> —1 Corinthians 13:4–8a (NIV 1984)

That is how God loves us and how we are to love others—and ourselves. Have you ever looked at how you view yourself in light of these verses? OCD screams at us, condemns us, and makes us do the most repetitive and draining compulsive tasks. Is that loving?

As I persevered in writing this book, I realized that ongoing freedom from the anxieties driving my OCD came from acknowledging both God's character and my character. When I was able to understand that I didn't always know what to do, I felt free to trust Christ. And I learned to rest in knowing that God is good, and that He truly does love me as His child—even more than a perfect parent could ever do. It is His love that casts out fear and ensures I am right with Him, not a to-do list. The fruit of love is freedom from fear. The truths that set us free—the truths that I write about throughout this book—are God's love and grace. The more we believe in and rely on His love and grace, the more freedom we will experience.

Let God's perfect love cast out all fear. It is my hope that this book helps our hearts come to know what our minds already know—that we are free in Christ, that His love for us will never fail, and that our relationship with Him is based on grace. These gifts are given to us completely independent of anything we could do to earn them.

CHAPTER 2

WHAT IT'S LIKE TO HAVE OCD – MY LIFE STORY

For the sake of those without OCD, I opened this book with the fictional story of Rachel to provide a picture of how intense OCD can feel and to illustrate the direct impact it can have on daily life. Although Rachel's story is fictional, the extreme emotional responses the character experiences mirror those of my past. Society often portrays OCD as funny, idiosyncratic behavior. Maybe there are some mild cases where laughter is the best cure. But for me and many OCD sufferers, this disorder means constantly battling feelings of insanity, desperation, and loneliness. One of my goals in this book is to sensitize those that care for OCD sufferers with some picture of the pain that OCDers endure, alone, within the walls of their own minds. This knowledge can make all the difference for OCD sufferers who, like all people, desperately want to be understood. The feelings of insanity, desperation, self-deprecating humor, isolation, and struggle just to get by have been very real to me. Every person is different and has a unique story, but for purposes of illustration, here is mine.

Childhood

Entangled String

Around the age of seven, I remember thinking there was an imaginary string attached to my back that I could never let get tangled. Worse yet, the string continued to unravel from my back as I walked. Therefore, if I walked around a tree, I had to make sure not to walk fully around it, or I would get "tied" to it. As you can imagine, this made recess a complicated time of the day. I constantly kept an eye on poles, trees, and even buildings, making sure I didn't get entangled to them. Getting ensnared was a very terrifying thought because it meant that I would have to get untangled. If I didn't quickly take care of the issue, I would have much more to untangle. Because of this, I tried to retrace my steps as soon as I felt entangled, which made the social aspects of school awkward and difficult.

Stuffed Animal Suffocation

My nanny, Marie, met her American husband during the Vietnam war and eventually moved to the US with him. Unfortunately, he left her, and she had to make a career for herself as a nanny. She was incredibly well-respected and even cared for the children of a famous congressman. After his children grew up, she began looking for another job, which is when my parents were introduced to her. They loved her and hired her right away. For years following Marie's first day, my mom would tell and re-tell the story of the first night she came home from work: "The house was immaculate! I couldn't believe it! Everything was in its place! Even the light in the entryway was dusted and sparkled!" And best of all, a home-cooked meal was ready. Marie's cooking was nothing short of amazing, and her work ethic was admirable. She was very mild-mannered and spoke softly with a strong

Vietnamese accent. My sister, brother, and I all loved her. She became part of the family.

Marie brought me a Christmas gift when I was eight years old. The following vignette reveals much about the struggles of my childhood and how a treasured gift could turn into an object of torment:

> "Thanks Marie!" I screamed as I grabbed the present. It was a small stuffed teddy bear, probably only eight inches long. *"Now, my big Kringle bear has a friend to sleep next to!"* I happily thought to myself.
>
> That night I took my tiny new bear upstairs and tucked him in next to Kringle. Kringle always had to be tucked in right up to his neck but not an inch further. I always "pretend" worried that he would suffocate if his face went under the covers—something that was rarely a problem because I usually fell asleep pretty quickly without moving around too much. I would begin dozing off, look over to make sure his head was still above the covers a few times, and be off to sleep within minutes.
>
> That night, however, I had two bears to put to sleep, with the newer one being much smaller than Kringle. I tucked them in, side by side. *"The new one should be closest to me,"* I supposed, for fear that he could get smothered without me ever knowing it if he was behind Kringle. *"OK, time to sleep, Mike,"* I told myself, noticing I was getting the uncomfortable feeling of worry. I shifted slightly—something that normally wouldn't have impacted Kringle's position. But much to my dismay, I noticed that the smaller bear was completely out of position.

As my anxiety increased, I repositioned the small bear. *"OK, now sleep,"* I told myself, and began dozing off. But I could not sleep. *"I have to readjust . . . No, I can't; the small bear might get smothered, and I'll have to reposition him. Just go to sleep, Mike!"* Two minutes pass. *"I really need to turn over! No, it's not worth it. But the bear won't be able to breathe! Oh man, I just need to sleep! Ugh, I have to turn over! No, I should sleep! That's it; I'm turning over. Oh no! He can't breathe!"*

After an hour or so of this, I'd eventually sense tiredness coming over me. *"This is your chance; fall asleep, Mike!"* I would demand of myself. But sensing the need to doze off before flipping over again didn't help the process of falling asleep. Finally, despite myself, sleep would eventually take over.

This went on nightly. Two weeks later, little had changed. *"OK, you know the drill,"* I would tell myself. *"You're almost asleep, just one more check of the small bear's head. But he has his back to me! No worries, you've done this before. You can shift your shoulders ever so slightly and then tilt your head as far as it can to the right; that will give you a clear look at little bear's face."* His position was great, and his body was neatly tucked underneath the covers. But the thoughts continued to bombard me. *"Wait, when I shifted my shoulders back to the left, did I mess up his position? Maybe I should look one more time. No, I'm sure he's fine. Remember? You had this exact same fear last night, and when you checked, he was still in a good position . . . Well, what if this time his body moved for some reason? I should check . . . No, don't*

> *check. Who am I kidding? I have to check!"* As I began tilting my shoulders slightly to the right I wondered if I felt the sheets move in a slightly different way than they had before. *"Shoot, did I drag my left foot? If I did, I probably shifted the sheets."*
>
> At this point I abandoned the delicate movements and aggressively flipped over to begin resituating both bears. I knew the consequences of this: an accelerated heart rate which would make it that much harder to sleep. Never mind the fact that the resituating process would leave me no more certain of little bear's safety than when I began. However, I knew I couldn't fall asleep given the level of doubt I had. I grabbed both bears and laid them down in their proper positions. Then I placed both sheets on top of them so only their heads were showing. *"Here comes the tricky part, Mike; you have to get under the covers without moving the bears at all."* I very slowly began moving the right portion of the covers over my body, trying my best to leave the left portion of the sheets unaffected. *"Should I try to face the bears this time? Mike, stop thinking about this and go to sleep! You're going to be so tired tomorrow."*

It was a gift that exhaustion took over my body on those nights. This particular obsessive-compulsive ritual often took more than an hour. It continued for months, possibly even a year or more.

The Hardy Boys

"Guys, let's go," Marie said as she opened the front door and ushered all three of us to the car. We were off to the library. Third grade was officially over, and it was very important to my parents that my brother and I do a lot of summer reading:

> When we got to the library, I came across the fictional mystery series, *The Hardy Boys*. I was immediately hooked and couldn't wait to dive in. The school had recommended that we read for a certain amount of time each day. When we returned home, I made my way to my brother's room and turned on the lamp before I lay down on his couch and started reading, loving the suspense and problem-solving on each page. But then, the cycle began.
>
> *"Shoot, I forgot to check exactly what time it was when I started reading. It's 11:05 a.m. right now, and I've probably been reading for five minutes. So, I'll assume it was 11 o'clock when I began."* I looked down and started reading again. I got about one or two sentences farther and looked at the clock again.
>
> *"It's 11:06 a.m. already! So, it was probably not 11 o'clock when I started. It was likely 11:01 a.m.—maybe even 11:02 a.m. I'll just use 11:02 a.m. to be safe. No, if I want to be totally safe, I should use 11:03 a.m. That will account for the interruptions I just had. I started reading at 11:03 a.m."*
>
> I looked down to start reading again, thrilled by every word on the page.
>
> "Mike, Marie is making a snack; do you want one?" my brother yelled from downstairs.
>
> "Sure!" I yelled back.
>
> "Like what?" he asked. I thought about it for a minute and then gave him a response. Then, I got up

and quickly went to the bathroom before making my way back to the couch.

"Great, I wasn't reading for the time that John asked the question. And I thought about what I wanted for a minute, plus the bathroom break."

I looked back at the clock; it read 11:17 a.m.

"Well, I started at 11:03 a.m., but I need to revise that to at least 11:04 a.m., so that when I finish reading, I can just subtract the time from the start time and know how long I've read. That's way easier than subtracting the end time from the beginning time, and then trying to subtract out all the breaks. But wait, 11:04 a.m. could easily be cheating. What if the conversation with John plus the bathroom break took three minutes? To be safe I should up the start time to 11:05 a.m. No, it could have taken longer. To be absolutely sure that I'm not padding my reading time, I will up the start time to 11:09 a.m. That allows five full minutes for the conversation with John and the bathroom break."

I felt completely dejected as I returned to my reading. I knew deep down that my break took a minute tops. But I had already shaved off three minutes from the start, plus another five.

I knew I was robbing myself of time I should have accounted for, but I didn't have any other option. The alternative was to use an earlier start time, but the idea of being guilt-ridden for potentially lying about my time was nowhere near worth it.

I eventually stopped counting altogether seeing that we didn't have to officially report anything to the school. If I remember correctly, I started telling my parents that I read "some" or "a lot" instead of reporting actual numbers.

Elementary School Confession

To describe my mom and dad's parenting style as protective would be an understatement. My maternal grandfather was born and raised in Egypt in the Coptic Orthodox Church. When he was 17, an evangelist from the US explained the gospel of salvation to him, which is completely by grace through faith, and he became a follower of Jesus. (See the Appendix for more about the promises of Christianity.) My grandfather went on to become an incredible pastor, author, and evangelist. He led a Baptist congregation and felt that we were to be set apart from many things in the culture, which is obviously part of becoming holy as we walk with God.

That was the atmosphere in which my mother grew up with her family in Egypt. Additionally, she was the bookworm of all bookworms, and keenly intelligent. She studied day and night. Excelling at school was a very high priority, and her life was even more sheltered because of it. After college and medical school, she and my father separately came to the United States in the mid-1970s, in large part to escape the hostility toward Christians in Egypt.

When they arrived in the US, they knew little to nothing about American culture and decided that protecting us from mainstream ideas was the best way to raise us. They strongly opposed sinful activity, but also many things that fell into the gray area of living the Christian life. Tattoos, men with long hair, rock and roll music, gambling, and drinking alcohol were forbidden. Not only that, but the atmosphere in our home suggested that we were to avoid people who practiced those behaviors as well. I assume they thought that the tighter the guardrails they built, the better.

As my struggle with OCD began to affect more areas of my life, I became hypersensitive to the people and things around me. I developed an obsession with pleasing my parents with respect to abstaining from things they thought were unacceptable or ungodly. If I could not completely avoid seeing something I knew they would frown upon, I felt compelled to confess it. More than 30 years later, I remember a specific confession, but there were many near identical ones that preceded and followed it:

> It was a sunny day in Great Falls, Virginia, where I attended elementary school. Looking back, an amazing amount of sunlight came through the windows, which made for a bright but also very hot classroom. I sat across from Lindsay who was very popular but soft-spoken. "Good morning," I said as we all sat down at the beginning of the day. As she usually did, she responded with a simple, "Hi," and started chatting softly to the girl seated next to her. I glanced down at her shirt, which had a huge picture printed on it. I was horrified; I immediately felt a pit in my stomach and looked away. I only caught a glimpse of the top portion of picture, but I was pretty certain I saw a man with long hair in the picture.
>
> *"Don't look! You know you aren't supposed to see things like that,"* I thought to myself. *"If you see that, you are going to have to confess. The day just started; the last thing you need is to see something you're not allowed to see, and then have to wait all day until your mom gets home at six o'clock so you can confess."*
>
> I was able to get through a good bit of time without seeing the image again. We eventually had to get up for an activity, and as we crossed paths, I

> saw the entire picture. It depicted the band "Guns N' Roses." So not only did I see long hair on a man, but I also saw a rock n' roll band!
>
> *"Great, Mike. You will definitely have to confess this."*
>
> After I got home, I had to wait three torturous hours for my mom to arrive. I don't remember what I did to pass the time. I probably watched an episode of *Batman* and tried to do some homework. When I heard the garage door open, my heart immediately raced.
>
> "Hi guys!" my mom said to my siblings and me as she came through the back door and into our living room. She was almost always very happy when she got home. Although she worked extremely hard, she loved her job, excelled at it, and seemed to have more than enough in the tank every night to meaningfully engage all of us.
>
> She made her way upstairs to her bedroom, and I followed right behind. Before she even got to the door, I quickly muttered, "Mom, a girl was wearing a shirt with a guy on it who had long hair and I saw it."
>
> "Oh, that's OK," she responded, not giving it another moment's thought. Instantly, I felt total relief and was able to go on with the rest of the evening.

As an adult, I can see this was a very common pattern to which I subjected myself. Hours of obsession about something I was either attempting to avoid or something I couldn't act on until later, followed by a very quick compulsion, followed by instant relief. The relief was, of course, short-lived, and the cycle of obsessing and acting on a resulting compulsion strengthened as it was repeated.

Looking back, my mom likely doesn't remember 99% of the times I "confessed" things to her, which I suppose I did dozens or even hundreds of times throughout my childhood. Her responses were always full of grace. Most of the time, she probably wasn't even paying enough attention to hear everything I was saying. All that mattered to me—or I should say all that mattered to my OCD—was that I received forgiveness for my actions.

Adolescence - High School

Freshman and Sophomore Years

My freshman year of high school is the most vivid memory I have of adolescence, as my walk with God soared to new heights. I basked in the presence of God for hours a day, sought His face, prayed prayers of thanks, and grieved for the lost. The experience was completely a gift from God. That year of my life was marked by the overwhelming presence of God, His grace, His companionship, His mercy, and His holiness. In that unique time of blessing, the overwhelming grace of God's presence nearly drowned out everything else. Nevertheless, OCD took its toll.

Sometimes, I would worry that I might have had a blasphemous thought while performing a task. Then, I would rebuke Satan and redo the very thing I was doing at the time the "blasphemous" thought occurred. At times it could take me 20 minutes to put my Bible back on the shelf after a time of prayer and reading. I would put it down, fear a blasphemous thought had entered my mind, rebuke Satan, take the Bible off the shelf, and finally put it back. The thought unavoidably resurfaced, so I would repeat the process dozens—maybe even hundreds—of times.

Explaining the agony of this experience with words is nearly impossible. John Bunyan wrote: "These things may seem ridiculous to others, even as ridiculous as they were in themselves, but to me they were most tormenting thoughts. Every one of them increased my misery."[1]

During that period, I would often take over half an hour to fall asleep at night. I would begin by getting ready for bed. Once in bed, I would pray to God for help, forgiveness, peace, joy, my lost friends, and so on. These prayers were sincere, and I had started doing them out of genuine love and relationship with the Lord. However, when I lay my head down to sleep, I would inevitably fear that I had just had a blasphemous thought toward God. I would immediately pray for forgiveness, but I felt an overwhelming sense of responsibility to sit up and put my hands together to pray.

Any opportunity to fall into a deep sleep would immediately be stolen, and I would begin an intense prayer for forgiveness, often followed by a verbal rebuke of Satan—something I was advised to do by my grandfather. At times, I would fear that I had indeed blasphemed God and was therefore in need of salvation; for surely a Christian would never blaspheme God. To ensure that I was saved, I would pray the sinner's prayer, ensuring I had included the essential elements of the faith. I would include a proclamation that I was a sinner, that Christ was born of the virgin Mary, that He was the Son of God, and that He died and rose again to give me salvation by faith. I would try to pray this prayer as fast as I could, knowing that a blasphemous thought was just around the corner, which if realized, would force me to rebuke Satan and start my prayers for forgiveness and salvation all over again. Even the fear that I had a blasphemous thought, let alone actually realizing one had crossed my mind, was enough to annihilate any sense of peace I may have had. I often would be up until two o'clock in the morning rebuking Satan and praying.

By my sophomore year of high school, the fear that I was not truly a Christian had crept into my life. Sure, I had experienced the presence of God and knew He was real, but the fear that my faith in Christ Himself was not genuine hounded my conscience nearly every day. Every time I *felt* that I doubted Christ or that my faith might somehow not be real, I would repeat the sinner's prayer. I had to make sure I knew that I was a Christian that very moment. As is the case with many OCD-related compulsions, this one came back minutes, sometimes even mere moments, later. Inevitably, I would end up repeating the prayer over and over again.

During this time, my mother took me to an unbelieving psychiatrist. He convinced me that I took my Bible reading and relationship with God too seriously and that I needed to relax. As a vulnerable teenager, I took his advice despite the peace, joy, and hope I had received in the presence of God. I remember often feeling sad, similar to the feeling of being in love with a woman yet thinking it was best not to speak to her. I wondered why this was the right thing to do. Unfortunately, I didn't question the psychiatrist's integrity or wisdom. So, I would pray continually as I had before in my everyday life, but I stopped reading and praying incessantly after school as I had previously done joyfully. This led to my feeling distant from God, and my walk with Him seemed to weaken over the next 12 to 18 months.

Fortunately, however, I had started taking a relatively high dose of Anafranil, which subdued the intensity of my OCD thought life and made daily life much more bearable. I eventually quit taking the medication because I was told that I couldn't run cross-country while taking Anafranil due to a minor heart condition. By God's grace, the intensity of OCD did not increase to an unbearable point until many years later.

Morning Rituals

When my brother was a junior and I was a freshman, we rode to school together every morning. Our schedules were full, as we were required to play a sport for at least two out of the three seasons, which meant many late nights of practice and study. He was very close to a straight-A student who literally spent over six hours studying every night. I ran cross-country, which included either a 5K race or running between four and six miles at practice every weekday after school. Add in that I am a night owl, and it's easy to see why I didn't like mornings, and OCD made the drag of mornings exponentially worse. My morning ritual went something like this:

> I awoke to a sermon by Charles Swindoll blasting through my alarm clock radio. I hit snooze, which was followed by my brother saying, "Mike, get up! We can't be late today!"
>
> I carefully got out of bed and made my way to the bathroom. I flipped on the light switch with the right hand side of my index finger of my right hand, closed the door with my right foot, and then very carefully started the process.
>
> *"Don't mess this up. Keep it as straightforward as possible; we are already late as it is,"* I thought to myself.
>
> I removed my t-shirt and folded it with the side that I had decided was most contaminated tucked as inward as possible—so that when I had to pick it up later, the chance of touching any potentially contaminated material would be minimized. I very carefully placed it on the floor, against the wall. I was *very* careful not to touch the wall in any way with my hands, because my hands were still considered contaminated since I hadn't washed them yet. Any contact between my hands and the wall would set off an entirely separate ritual, and there was no time for that.

I then removed my sweatpants and followed the same logic. I was satisfied with the fold this time. Then came the underwear. The intense feeling of potential contamination was lower compared to the sweats and t-shirt. All I had to do was ensure that the backside was facing out, before folding my underwear into thirds and placing it on top of the shirt.

I made my way to the sink. The knobs were round and were meant to be turned using one's fingers. However, since I considered my fingers dirty, I made a tight fist and used the side farthest from my thumb to push down hard on the knob and twist it. My thinking was that the side of the hand was "less contaminated" than my fingertips for two reasons. One was that I had just used them to fold the contaminated clothing, and the second was because I believed that the body produced far less oil on the side of the hand.

As with everyone's OCD, mine had rules that could not be broken, but my mind was able to find loopholes to make getting through life a possibility. One loophole that helped immensely was that if a non-greasy part of my body touched an object, then that object would only have secondary contamination. Don't misunderstand me; it would still be contaminated—but not as contaminated as the contaminated part of my body that touched it. The benefit came from the rule of tertiary contamination, which I defined as the object or body part that touched secondarily contaminated objects. I had somehow become convinced that tertiary contamination was "acceptable." In this example, my fingers were considered directly contaminated, as they had produced natural oils during the night.

However, since the side of my fist was considered less oily, I could consider the level of contamination on the sink handle to be at a secondary level. Therefore, as long as there was no oil—or perceived oil—on my hands, I could turn the faucet on again in the future, use it, and turn it off. Even though my hand would be wet at that point, it would be oil-free, so my washed hand only had tertiary-level contamination once it touched the knob. Simple and straightforward, right?

Once my hands were clean, I could breeze through brushing my teeth and turning the water off. Then came the most daunting and miserable part of my morning. I turned the shower water on to a pretty hot temperature, got in, closed the curtain with what were still clean hands, and began the process. I looked down at the pile of rough washcloths and sighed. First, I rinsed my body with high pressure water. Then I grabbed a bar of soap, lathered my hands, and washed specific areas with my bare hands.

In my mind, this left my hands at a high level of contamination. My heart rate increased because of the precision required in this next phase. As I began to rinse my hands off, I became abundantly aware of where all the "contaminated" water was splashing off my hands, first on the shower walls and then on the shower curtain. Thankfully, the magnet at the bottom of the shower curtain held it against the tub close enough to the wall that contaminated water could not escape outside the tub. If it had not worked, I would have had to address that after the shower using less proven methods, which would have taken much more time.

Once the initial hand rinse was complete, I grabbed the bar of soap and began lathering my hands as much as possible. The thought here was not to clean my hands, but to remove enough layering of the soap to the point that I was convinced I was using a layer of the soap that I considered "non-contaminated." I don't remember the exact indicators for determining whether enough of the bar had been removed to be considered clean. It had to do with the physical appearance of the bar of soap—either a change in how light reflected off it or recognition that it had gotten physically smaller than when I picked it up.

Once I was convinced the bar was rid of all contamination, I rinsed my hands off and then washed them with the "clean" bar of soap. I then grabbed the first washcloth, which was folded in quarters and soaked it in water. I lathered the top side of the cloth by scrubbing the soap across it three times before putting it down. Once I was done scrubbing, I folded the quartered cloth in half the other way and used the "less contaminated" side to scrub the same area again. I then squeezed the washcloth as dry as possible by ringing it multiple times and placed it in the far corner of the side of the tub adjacent to the wall.

"Mike, hurry up!" I heard my brother yell.

"OK, I will!" I yelled back, knowing that my idea of rushing would be very inadequate given what was left to do.

I repeated the same process several more times with the additional washcloths, noticing that my anxiety from contamination lessened with each one. However, knowing that I was making my brother and sister late for school made the logical part of my brain more anxious.

Finally, convinced my body was clean, I had to make sure I rinsed all the contaminated water off the shower walls and curtains. I did this by grabbing the shower head and turning it as far to the left and then to the right as possible, watching the water cascade down the walls and curtain. I would hit the button so that the shower water was redirected from the head to the bottom nozzle before I opened the shower curtain. The end of the process was near, but I had to make sure this next step didn't cause any major delays.

The soles of my feet were still considered dirty. I don't know why my feet followed different rules; they just did. They didn't have to be scrubbed with soap. Rather, they had to be adequately rinsed with clean water. To execute this most effectively, I did what I had learned led to the highest rate of success. I turned my body so that my front faced the outside of the shower. I lifted my left leg and placed my foot under the running water. Just in case some of the contaminated water streamed off the base of my foot and onto my ankle or lower shin, I slid my leg toward the inside wall of the tub so that I rinsed off about one-third of my shin. I then moved my foot away from the running water, let it drip for a few seconds, lifted my foot over the side of the tub, and turned my body 180 degrees while placing my left foot on the bathmat outside the shower. From there, I immediately turned back around so my front faced the shower wall, being careful to not allow my right foot to leave the tub. I then lifted my right leg and placed my right foot under the running water, repeating the same process as I had with my left foot. This required pretty good balance, because my waist was outside the tub, which required that I lean forward to maintain balance while holding my right leg far enough back that it stayed under the running water. Even though the tub was now considered clean (from the rinse I performed after using the last washcloth), the bottom was still contaminated, so slipping and having a toe or a portion of the right foot touch the tub bottom was not an option. After the rinse, I placed my right foot outside the tub. I now considered myself "non-contaminated" from head to foot.

My brother begrudgingly informed me that the process had taken 40 minutes. But I wasn't anywhere near finished.

Although I had gone through all the necessary processes correctly, the soles of my feet were contaminated again. This didn't catch me off guard, because I knew that was inevitable and had become part of the ritual. I went through my intricate process as best I could until I was fully dressed, knowing that I wouldn't manage to do it perfectly. (I kept a strict mental log of any minor contaminations from this point forward and addressed them once I had a free minute at school.)

I quickly put my socks and shoes on and then ran to the bathroom. The steam had mostly made its

> way out since it had been a solid four or five minutes since I left. I carefully placed one hand under the sweatpants and put the other on top of my underwear. I picked the pile up and held it as far away from my body as possible without extending my arms too far, which would cause contact with the wall. I quickly took the clothes to my hamper and dropped them in, ran back to the bathroom, and washed my hands using the side-of-fist method to turn the water on.
>
> I grabbed my backpack and ran downstairs. My brother was waiting at the kitchen table. He used to get upset at me for being late, but at some point he loosened up and didn't mention it as much. Either he thought he was being too hard on me, or he realized that nothing he could say or do would ever make me be on time.

I knew my morning tardiness was completely unacceptable, and being the people pleaser that I am, I felt terrible every day. There were no exceptions to my tardiness. I think the earliest we ever made it to school that year was five minutes late, but more often, we were 15 to 25 minutes late. Years later, I learned that my siblings had no idea the toll that OCD was taking on me. They knew I had it, but they had no comprehension of the extent to which it affected my everyday life—let alone my spiritual life.

Did Satan Just Help Me?!

I often struggled with the thought of "*Oh no, I think Satan helped me*" do this or that. For example, when trying to remember someone's name, people often take a moment to think and try to remember locations or events or faces that might help jog their memory. However, whenever I would do this and successfully remember something, I would often have the fear that I had somehow asked for Satan's help. Rebuking Satan verbally often followed as soon I could do so in private.

The same was true for trying to find something that was lost, even if it was merely a pair of socks. Therefore, if I indeed found the socks, I would feel terrible for having found them.

The most aggravating experiences occurred when this obsession interrupted a time-sensitive event. During cross-country races in high school, I would often have thoughts such as, *"Did I just ask Satan to help me not trip on that crack or pass someone or run a bit faster?"* The compulsion was to stop running, rebuke Satan under my breath, and ask God for forgiveness. I would then pause for the amount of time I thought I had supposedly gained before I continued running. I don't remember how often I stopped during races, but I do remember having a good bit of victory and not giving in to this compulsion after a while. But this did not stop the thoughts from wreaking havoc on my mind during the races.

I later learned that I wasn't alone. One of the fastest marathon runners in US history, Jeff Wells, who holds both Master of Theology and Doctor of Ministry degrees, had nearly identical thoughts, which he describes in *Breaking Free of OCD: My Battle with Mental Pain and How God Rescued Me.*[2]

Matthew 5:23–24 and Communion

It was a beautiful spring or summer morning and the first Sunday of the month. When we arrived at church, I saw the communion dishes at the front of the auditorium. Our family sat very close to the front that day, and I distinctly remember looking straight up at the podium.

Before communion started, a man got up to speak. His name was Paul. He was a towering six-foot-seven aspiring preacher who was in his early to mid-twenties, a member of our church who had been chosen to speak about preparing our hearts for communion. He referenced Matthew 5:23–24, which states, "*Therefore if you bring your gift to the altar, and there remember that your brother has something against you, leave your gift there before the altar, and go your way. First be reconciled to your brother, and then come and offer your gift.*"

With conviction, Paul spoke of an altercation that he had with a friend and said he had felt led to call the man and reconcile the issue. He had ignored it for a while, but told us with sincerity, "I remember praying to God one day, and He distinctly told me, 'You are not going to be any closer to Me until you make it right with that man,' so I stopped praying right then and called him."

Soon after this story, the message started wreaking havoc on my life. In the years that followed, even well into adulthood, I would get incredibly anxious whenever I saw that communion was going to be given. Many times, I feared that someone would have something against me, no matter how minor. I would then decide to skip the plate and juice when they were passed to me. This was embarrassing, of course, as others around knew me, and I'm sure they wondered why I wasn't partaking.

Later in my college years, this message and passage would cause so much strain on me that I felt socially crippled, as I will discuss in a later chapter.[i]

---

i. In a story of redemption, this very same Paul became the pastor of the young adult ministry where I met my wife. During our few years attending that ministry, I got to know Paul quite well. This helped remove the negative association and burden I had felt when first listening to him over ten years prior.

Adulthood

The Weirdest Apology Ever

During my junior year of college, a group of about 20 people from our church went down to Daytona Beach during spring break. We spent most days at the beach and spent our nights playing games, hanging out, or doing things like playing miniature golf.

The late mornings were particularly mellow after breakfast was over. If it was too early to head to the beach, we would spend a lot of time hanging out where we were staying. About 15 of us had rented a place that had a few rooms and a big living area with a kitchen and two or three couches. One morning I was talking with my roommate, Matt, and a couple of other friends when a guy named Jason walked in with his girlfriend, Melissa. I didn't know them all that well, and for some reason I was a bit intimidated by them—either because I felt they were in the "in" crowd, or maybe just because they were a very quiet couple, and I often felt judged by quiet types since I tended to be loud and talkative.

I think I waved to them as they walked through the front door, and they started a conversation with a couple of other people on the other side of the room. I soon turned my back to them and continued my conversation with Matt and the others. At one point I noticed that my shirt wasn't tucked into my jeans. The living area put us in a somewhat awkward position. On one hand, I felt like I was in my "house" and even in my room, because the entire arrangement was informal and laid back. However, there were others in the room I didn't know that well, including a female. In the end, I decided that it would be OK to tuck in my shirt right then and there. To do so, I unbuckled my jeans and undid my zipper about halfway so that I could tuck in my shirt, before quickly zipping my jeans back up and tightening my belt.

The entire process probably took less than five seconds, and there is a good chance no one even noticed. However, there was the possibility that others did notice—including Melissa. I realized that my action could have been very offensive and inappropriate. Still, I didn't think much of it for quite some time.

When we finally got back to our dorm at Virginia Tech, I remember reading the Bible and coming across Matthew 5:23-24, which again says: "*Therefore if you bring your gift to the altar, and there remember that your brother has something against you, leave your gift there before the altar, and go your way. First be reconciled to your brother, and then come and offer your gift.*" I was very well acquainted with these verses, because of the condemnation associated with it from my youth. Reflecting on this passage, I felt strongly condemned when I thought about the way I had unzipped my jeans in front of Jason and his girlfriend. If Melissa had seen, she and Jason could have been terribly offended. I thought:

> *"You had to go and be soooo cute, didn't you? Why were you so stupid and reckless as to undress yourself in front of a female, who is a Christian no less! If ever a brother has something against you, it is right now. If Jason saw you tuck your shirt in that way while his girlfriend was in the room—or worse yet—if she saw it and told him, then he must be very offended."*

I shared these thoughts with my two closest friends, Matt, who was there when the episode took place and Tim who lived next door. They were both well aware of my OCD and tried to help me navigate my thoughts.

"I have to email Jason and apologize," I insisted. "He could potentially be so offended."

"Mike, don't do that! You better not do that. That is literally a crazy thing to do," they both retorted. "Besides, there is no way he will have any idea of what you are even talking about."

"Yeah, I see your point," I said, deciding then and there that they were right.

However, the next time I picked up my Bible to read and pray, I was hounded by condemnation and thinking, *"Mike, you can't just ignore a passage in the Bible. If there is even the slightest chance that you offended Jason or Melissa, you need to make it right."*

I was older and experienced enough with OCD to know that Matt and Tim had steered me right, but I chose to give in to my compulsions. I logged onto my computer, opened my email and started a draft. The next five minutes were spent sending an email to Jason. I didn't know Melissa at all, so I planned on sending the email to him only.

"I cannot believe I'm doing this! Mike, you have to stop." I could feel a pit in my stomach because I knew that if I sent the email, it would lead to one of the most awkward situations of my life—which is really saying something.

But I continued typing: "Jason, it was great getting to know you during spring break last month. The volleyball tournament was fun."

"And . . . here we go. If we are going to jump off a cliff, at least do it fast," I told myself. I continued, "Anyway, I wanted to write and apologize for something you may not have even noticed. One of the days you came over to our room during our trip to Daytona, I realized my shirt was untucked, so I decided to tuck it in. To do so I undid my zipper, and my underwear may have been showing. I want to apologize for how inappropriate that was if it made you feel uncomfortable."

My thoughts churned: *"Mike, you are truly insane. Stop explaining!!!"* But I continued typing: "Worse yet, there is chance Melissa saw all that happen! If she did, please let her know that I am sorry for offending her."

My mind was warring against itself. *"It's one thing to draft the email; it's another to send it! Do not hit Send!"*

But if I do hit Send, I reasoned, I will be able to read my Bible and pray without any hindrance to my relationship with God. Matthew 5:23–24 won't be hanging over my head. *"But Mike, don't; this is truly insane."*

I think I held the mouse over the Send button as I contemplated what to do. Matt and Tim weren't around to stop me, so I sat in turmoil for a bit and finally hit Send.

"What a relief! I can pray again and be at peace! Mike, you are such an idiot. I cannot believe you just did that! What is Jason going to do? Not respond? Or respond and tell you that you're crazy? Tell no one? Tell everyone you know and their brother?"

The feeling I experienced next was a major part of finding victory over OCD. In addition to the rush of adrenaline I felt for doing something so insane, the embarrassment, regret, and disappointment in myself was something similar to sadness. For years, I had known in my head that what I had just done was merely a compulsion performed in order to assuage an obsession. That was nothing new. But for the first time, I clearly felt *in my heart* that what I had done was not God's will. It was not a reasonable thing to do. It was not an act that brought me or others closer to Him or one that glorified Him. It was confusing, embarrassing for both parties, and not done with a sound mind.

Ironically, that feeling gave me freedom. For the first time, I was convinced in my heart of what my head already knew. From that day forward, every time Matthew 5:23–24 entered my mind and I was tempted to apologize for phantom grievances, I would remember that moment and realize that I was likely not seeing the entire picture. Yes, there would always be the .01% chance that God wanted me to apologize for something, but I could refer back to this moment, when it was so clear to my heart that apologizing was not God's will. There was a much greater chance I was about to relive the experience I had when I emailed Jason. This "epiphany" may seem so obvious to most people reading this, but to me it was a groundbreaking tool I finally had to combat my obsessions.[ii]

I also believe this experience was the first time I realized that the hardest thing to do is not always the right thing to do. Life usually teaches us the opposite. For example, those who win a race have often trained harder than everyone else. The same is true of academic success, promotions at work, having the best-kept home, or being the best at one's craft. I realize that this general truth had crept into my OCD thought life: The harder or more daunting a compulsion, the more "right" it seemed. What a terrible lie to believe! Compulsions that are the most difficult to act on are based on OCD obsessions just as much as easy compulsions. Even worse was the belief that fulfilling the most difficult compulsions was the most honorable way to live. This definitely had a negative impact on my view of God's character and my beliefs about His view of me.

And in case you were wondering, Jason wrote me back a day later with a one-liner to the effect of, "Hey Mike, thanks for your email. Don't worry about it; we're all good." We never spoke again, which I kind of expected. I'm hoping he somehow discovers this book so he can finally understand why he got such an insane email!

Michael Jordan Photos

It was a weeknight in the winter of 2002. I pulled up to my co-worker Rui's apartment complex. Rui was from Portugal and had been a very serious martial artist when he was younger, having finished sixth in a world event. He was incredibly mild-mannered and soft-spoken, which amazed me and his boss in light of his accolades as a fighter.

---

ii. See Chapter 4, "Logic Solvers," for more on this topic.

We spent a few minutes getting ready and quickly headed to my car for our 90-minute drive to Washington, DC to see Michael Jordan play during his two-year stint with the Washington Wizards . . . *the* Michael Jordan. Even better, I was still very involved in sports photography and was considering a career change. I had brought my best camera and lens to the game but knew I likely wouldn't get anything portfolio-worthy because we could only get nosebleed tickets. Most home games were sold out since fans were aware there weren't many more chances to see "MJ" play.

It wasn't until we got to our seats that I realized how high up nosebleed tickets were in that arena. But Rui and I were still excited to be there. We couldn't clearly see the individual players, but we could definitely identify MJ. He was the best or second-best player on the floor despite being 39 years old and just coming back from a three-year retirement. He still had the same swagger and style of play, although his ability to fly and glide wasn't what it had been. I used my zoom lens and started taking photos despite being so far away from the action.

Although it was a weeknight, we were still surprised when the crowd began to thin out as the game wore on. In the third quarter, we started talking about sneaking down to the more expensive seats. By the start of the fourth quarter, we decided to make our move.

I felt a little uneasy doing this, but I couldn't let the opportunity to see MJ up close pass me by. As we headed down the stairs, we were both pleasantly surprised by the ease with which we were able to get access to amazing seats. We settled in about ten rows behind the rim where MJ was scoring! At risk of dating myself, I have to admit I was still using a 35 mm film camera. Each roll had 36 exposures and cost a few dollars to develop. Knowing how rare the opportunity was, I shot away—frame after frame at high speed whenever he had the ball. I brought enough rolls of film in case we got an opportunity like this. And then the moment came.

Jordan got a pass down low and went up to dunk—right in front of us! I shot away, at around 3.5 frames per second, which wasn't all that bad back then. Of course, I was thrilled that I was sitting so close, but I wouldn't know whether any shots came out until I got the film developed.

Days later, I finally got my negatives back and hurriedly scanned through them. As I got to the play leading to the dunk, I noticed that some shots were out of focus. As I progressed toward the frames where MJ went airborne, one shot really stuck out. I had gotten it, his tongue hanging out and all. The shot was in focus; there was intensity showing on his face, and to top it off, he was clearly getting fouled. I was beyond ecstatic; I got the negative printed as soon as possible. It all turned out so well.

But that wasn't the end of it. Within a few days, the condemnation began: "*Mike, you know better. Sneaking down to the more expensive seats is essentially stealing. You didn't pay to sit where you took the picture, so you don't deserve to have the picture.*"

Such thoughts in and of themselves were not atypical for me, and I was able to carry the weight of them for a few days. But the cycle continued.

I started to feel that I was a thief, undeserving of a relationship with God. Praying and reading my Bible felt out of reach. And that was even before I started to think about the team's name. The Wizards! I was supporting a team with a name associated with witchcraft.

About four or five weeks later, I continued to try to ignore the thoughts, which by this time had greatly intensified. I vividly remember trying to read God's Word and take notes when the thoughts entered full attack mode:

> "*You are at risk of being deceived. Don't forget that you essentially stole when you sneaked down to the nice seats. Plus, you are supporting a team that has an*

> *evil mascot. You are potentially living in such a state of sin and deception that there is no guarantee your reading of the Word will be interpreted properly. You need to make sure you rid yourself of possibly being under evil deception. Even if the risk is tiny, you need to do all you can to remove the .01% chance you are being deceived."*

As I tried to move on to pray and read my Bible, the thoughts overcame any sense of peace or stability I had. It became clear that I needed to do something in order to ensure I had fully "repented" of my sins.

First, I needed to call Ticketmaster and confess what I did. I decided I could make things right by telling them where my original seat was, the location of the seat I took without paying, and to ask for the price difference between the two seats. Then I could pay the difference and know I had repented of theft.

Second and much more tortuous, I had to disassociate and denounce any and all support of the Washington Wizards. How could supporting a team that finds witchcraft "cute" enough to be a mascot be an organization I could connect with in any way? Wasn't I at risk of being deceived by evil? To disassociate and denounce the team, I was convinced I had to stop watching their games. And then came the gut-wrenching thought: I also had to destroy all my photos of MJ, since he played for the Wizards.

> *"Mike, you have to do these things immediately. You think you should pray about this, do you? How do you know that you aren't so deep into deception that your decision to pray isn't actually Satan tricking you to stop you from doing what you need to do? If you pray, you are at risk of falling straight into Satan's web*

of lies. Don't dig any deeper holes. Go do what you have to do to repent; then come back and pray and read the Bible once you have repented of all potentially deceptive influences."

At this point, I confided in my mother, as I lived less than 90 minutes away and visited home most weekends. She did what she could to comfort me and talk me through my thoughts. She also was wise enough to take the negatives of MJ and hide them. She was not going to let me give in to my compulsions.

I then made my way back to my bedroom and tried to start reading my Bible, but condemning thoughts continued to race.

"Wait, even if you no longer have the chance to destroy the photos since they are hidden; even if you think it might be OK not to call Ticketmaster to confess and pay the difference in ticket prices, what makes you think you can just start reading the Bible again? All the passages you've read between the basketball game and now are potentially twisted and misunderstood in your brain. So that means that all your Bible reading for the last four weeks could have been done while living with an unrepentant heart. Therefore, your understanding of all those verses could have been twisted under the cloud of evil deception. If you want to remove the chance of deception altogether, you will have to remember all the passages you've read in the last four weeks and reread them now that the "veil" of potential deception has been removed."

The idea of rereading all the passages I had read over the last four weeks was daunting. Despite this mental attack, I had been reading quite a bit and remembering all the passages that needed to be reread was literally impossible.

I must point out that at that time, I did not consider these thought patterns irrational. I was aware that the entire idea of being deceived was absurd and had way less than a one in a trillion chance of being true. The issue I could not get over was that there was *a* chance, no matter how small. If a path existed that could remove the chance altogether, then I had to follow it.

Unanswered Phone Calls

Throughout my life and into adulthood, my late maternal grandfather was exceedingly kind and patient with me as the manifestations of my OCD were often placed on him. We had countless conversations regarding theological issues that were torturing me with anxiety and fear of condemnation. If there was a consequence to be had, I was determined to find it and make sure there was a zero percent chance I could somehow be in position to bear the consequence.

I would call my grandfather for explanations of the verses in question in hopes that he would *not* answer. That is not a typo. I wanted so badly to just take care of my end of controlling the situation, which was to call and see if he was available to answer my questions. Of course, there were times that I really did want him to pick up and assuage my fears, but other times I just wanted to do what I needed to do in order to absolve myself of further responsibility. My thought process went something like this: *"Well, I may be in horrible trouble with respect to my standing with God, and all I know to do is ask my grandfather for an explanation of my fears. As long as I ask, I'll have done all I can do."*

Even if he didn't answer the phone and give me an explanation in those instances, I had neutralized my anxiety by doing the compulsion, for I had done the only thing I could do to control the situation. I somehow knew that I didn't need him to answer a question he had likely answered before; I just needed to control what I could on my end. I now realize how much of his time and attention he lovingly gave to me in my most frenetic OCD moments. The patience he showed me as I asked about the same fears over and over, and clearly sometimes for no other reason than compulsion, was truly an act of unconditional love.

Unfortunately, these last two stories detail just a tiny portion of my many mental battles with condemnation. Christian OCD sufferers will no doubt relate to my stories of fearing God's wrath for driving a mile above the speed limit because of the urging of Romans 13 to submit to governing authorities, or being stricken by a painful panic attack because I feared I had confused the name of Jesus with that of Satan, and so on. For OCD sufferers, especially those who are believers, it is common to experience the fear of condemnation so acutely that we fabricate instances in which we may have done something egregious enough to earn condemnation, despite the fact that we have been redeemed by a Savior who sets us free from bondage to sin, condemnation, and death. Fortunately, my mother was able to help me through this incredibly hard time, and this low point convinced me to finally seek out a Christian psychiatrist.

Now and the Future

I have often felt pressure both from myself and others to be completely symptom-free before publishing this book—the idea being that I must be entirely victorious before I share what I've learned about coping with this disease. And although I have faith that God can rid me of this disorder at any moment and for all of time, that day has not yet come. However, my ability to fight through and cope with the many ways this disorder attacks me is superior to what it was 35 years ago. I have tried to convey the lessons I learned along the way, and my hope is that the following chapters give you some weapons to use in your fight as well.

Being forced to continually rely on God's grace during times of fragility has kept me grounded. It leads me to acknowledge God as my constant and daily provider of literally everything—from the air I breathe to the sanity I have. In the same way that Apostle Paul was given a thorn in the flesh to prevent him from being exalted beyond measure, I believe God still gives thorns to us as believers so we rely on His grace and see His strength made perfect in our weakness. As long as I must bear this disorder, I believe God wants me to say, as Apostle Paul said: *"I take pleasure in infirmities, in reproaches, in needs, in persecutions, in distresses, for Christ's sake. For when I am weak, then I am strong"* (2 Corinthians 12:10).

CHAPTER 3

WHY DOES GOD ALLOW OCD?

What could make years of torment, embarrassment, broken relationships, and the heavy burden of relentless, obsessive thoughts have meaning? Why? Why, you may ask, does it have to be so difficult just to get through the day? Why does a task as simple as washing my hands or locking my door or praying to God have to be so arduous that it seems unbearable?

Ultimately, it is natural to ask why God allows OCD. And on a personal level, it is natural to ask why God allows us to suffer this private torment. The key to gaining wisdom in this regard is to recognize how great, good, just, and righteous our God is. Our ways and thoughts are not His. Our perspective is mired in the present and limited by our restricted knowledge and understanding. Yet God is omniscient, omnipresent, omnipotent, and eternal. Even so, God shares in our sufferings, knows our struggles intimately, and has a greater plan to use our struggles for our own good.

God's Ways Are Not Our Ways

The Case for Faith by Lee Strobel explains the dilemma this way:

> Imagine a bear in a trap and a hunter who, out of sympathy, wants to liberate him. He tries to win the bear's confidence, but he can't do it, so he has to shoot the bear full of drugs. The bear, however, thinks this is an attack and that the hunter is trying to kill him. He doesn't realize that this is being done out of compassion.
>
> Then, in order to get the bear out of the trap, the hunter has to push him further into the trap to release the tension on the spring. If the bear were semiconscious at that point, he would be even more convinced that the hunter was his enemy who was out to cause him suffering and pain. But the bear would be wrong. He reaches this incorrect conclusion because he's not a human being.[1]

Now, I am confident this analogy is applicable to how we often perceive and respond to God. When trials come, some argue the following: "God is supposed to be good, yet because bad things happen and difficulties exist, and I don't know why, I conclude that either God does not exist or that He is not good." This reflects a temporal and limited perspective. It would be as if we stared at a complex building, and because we did not fully understand how it was made, we deny its existence or question its soundness. We would never do that; rather, we marvel at the architect for their work.

> *"For My thoughts are not your thoughts, nor are your ways My ways," says the LORD. "For as the heavens are higher than the earth, so are My ways higher than your ways, and My thoughts than your thoughts."*
>
> —Isaiah 55:8–9

God Plays by His Own Rules

When our pain tempts us to view God as distant or callous to our suffering, we must remember that He loved us so much that He willingly sacrificed fellowship with His one and only Son for the forgiveness of our sins, which makes our arguments against His goodness all the more absurd. It would be one thing if God was untouched by pain and asked us to endure it. On the contrary, Christ's separation from the Father is a pain we will not understand this side of heaven. Remember too that Christ endured more pain than we have ever been asked to bear and was called a man of sorrows and acquainted with grief (Isaiah 53:3). He intimately understands the pain and suffering we endure in these bodies and sympathizes with our weaknesses. Matthew 26:36–39 gives us an inside look at how Jesus felt prior to being crucified:

> *Then Jesus came with them to a place called Gethsemane, and said to the disciples, "Sit here while I go and pray over there." And He took with Him Peter and the two sons of Zebedee, and He began to be sorrowful and deeply distressed. Then He said to them, "My soul is exceedingly sorrowful, even to death. Stay here and watch with Me." He went a little farther and fell on His face, and prayed, saying, "O My Father, if it is possible, let this cup pass from Me; nevertheless, not as I will, but as You will."*

The crucifixion demonstrates the ultimate sacrifice. Not only did our Savior suffer, but God the Father also faced separation from His Son for our sake. The Creator of the universe allowed His only begotten Son to die a horrible death so that we could live. We should be encouraged knowing that our obedience and faith in God's plan in times of great sorrow and distress shadows that of our Savior and pleases God. So, when God asks us to trust and believe Him even when we struggle, we can rest knowing that He, too, experienced unimaginable pain so that we could be in relationship with Him.

Our Struggles Can Refine and Strengthen Us

We can acknowledge that God uses our trials to strengthen us. For the person who battles OCD, believing God is good is the equivalent of pushing a boulder uphill. God asks us to believe He is good and that He works everything together for our good. Our challenge, as demonstrated in the example of the boulder below, is to cling—by faith—to the truth that God is faithful.

> Once upon a time, there was a man who was sleeping at night in his cabin when suddenly his room filled with light and the Saviour appeared. The Lord told the man He had work for him to do, and showed him a large rock in front of his cabin. The Lord explained that the man was to push against the rock with all his might. This the man did, day after day. For many years he toiled from sun up to sun down, his shoulders set squarely against the cold, massive surface of the unmoving rock, pushing with all his might.
>
> Each night the man returned to his cabin sore and worn out, feeling that his whole day had been spent in vain. Seeing that the man was showing signs of discouragement, Satan decided to enter the picture placing thoughts into the man's mind such as: "You

have been pushing against that rock for a long time, and it hasn't budged. Why kill yourself over this? You are never going to move it." Thus giving the man the impression that the task was impossible and that he was a failure.

These thoughts discouraged and disheartened the man even more. "Why kill myself over this?" he thought. "I'll just put in my time, giving just the minimum of effort and that will be good enough." And that he planned to do until one day he decided to make it a matter of prayer and take his troubled thoughts to the Lord.

"Lord," he said, "I have laboured long and hard in your service, putting all my strength to do that which you have asked. Yet, after all this time, I have not even budged that rock a half a millimeter. What is wrong? Why am I failing?" To this the Lord responded compassionately, "My child, when long ago I asked you to serve me and you accepted, I told you that your task was to push against the rock with all your strength, which you have done. Never once did I mention to you that I expected you to move it. Your task was to push.

And now you come to me, your strength spent, thinking that you have failed. But, is that really so? Look at yourself. Your arms are strong and muscled, your back sinewed and brown, your hands are callused from constant pressure, and your legs have become massive and hard. Through opposition, you have grown much and your abilities now surpass that which you used to have. Yet you haven't moved

> the rock. But your calling was to be obedient and to push and to exercise your faith and trust in My wisdom. This you have done. I, my child, will now move the rock."[2] [iii]

These things are so hard to believe when OCD is causing us so much pain. I know, I have been there with bleeding hands, ruined relationships, fear of insanity, and overwhelming hopelessness. But you and I must remember this: If God is allowing OCD in our lives, it's not because He's vindictive or callous toward our pain. Rest knowing that when you struggle with OCD, God will use it to produce endurance so you may be complete, lacking in nothing. These words are more encouraging to me than most. The most difficult times of coping with OCD are not when I feel defeated or in a rut, but when I feel that it's all useless, pointless, and will never lead to anything beneficial. However, God knows everything we go through and asks that we trust Him, no matter how much pain we endure, or how senseless we feel our suffering is at times.

Although she veered theologically later in life, Hannah Whitall Smith eloquently describes this circumstance:

> One of the most fatal things in the life of faith is discouragement; one of the most helpful is confidence. A very wise man once said that in overcoming temptations confidence was the first thing, confidence the second, and confidence the third. We

---

iii. See Chapter 5 for more on the difference between a trial and the testing of your faith. Also, it is worth mentioning that both this section and Chapter 5 talk about faith in God who is our Heavenly Father. In no way is there any implication that one's salvation is dependent on their ability to maintain the correct frame of mind about God's goodness in the midst of their struggle.

> must expect to conquer. That is why the Lord said so often to Joshua, "Be strong and of a good courage"; "Be not afraid, neither be thou dismayed"; "Only be thou strong and very courageous." And it is also the reason He says to us, "Let not your heart be troubled, neither let it be afraid." The power of temptation is in the fainting of our own hearts. The enemy knows this well, and always begins his assaults by discouraging us, if he can in any way accomplish it.[3]
>
> *My brethren, count it all joy when you fall into various trials, knowing that the testing of your faith produces patience. But let patience have its perfect work, that you may be perfect and complete, lacking nothing.*
>
> —James 1:2–4

Applying this verse can help when it comes to pain and anguish in our lives. We don't know why things happen, but we do know God is good and true to His Word. His grace has been, and will continue to be, sufficient. Notice the verse does not say that His grace will remove all struggle and pain. But He will be there, pouring out His grace on us, and it will be sufficient to carry us through. If life for a Christ-follower is about growing closer to God, then OCD has been one of my biggest gifts because it has forced me to remain humble and rely only on Him and His daily strength. I can build my own world using my talents, but that is not how God makes us Christlike. If you have OCD, don't be bitter at God; don't give up on God. He is using every struggle for your good. Don't ever stop believing this and ask for faith in times of unbelief. He knows we are from the dust and that we are weak and feeble and wayward. That is why we have Christ, our Shepherd, and the Holy Spirit.

> *You are of God, little children, and have overcome them, because He who is in you is greater than he who is in the world.*
>
> —1 John 4:4

Our Struggle Can Help Others

> *Blessed be the God and Father of our Lord Jesus Christ, the Father of mercies and God of all comfort, who comforts us in all our tribulation, that we may be able to comfort those who are in any trouble, with the comfort with which we ourselves are comforted by God. For as the sufferings of Christ abound in us, so our consolation also abounds through Christ.*
>
> —2 Corinthians 1:3–5

My wife struggles from anxiety at times. I have found that God somehow orchestrated our relationship in such a way that we can relate to, empathize with, and encourage one another. Better yet, we are able to give each other insight into why we might be stumbling into anxiety. This is something neither of us would have benefited from had I not struggled with OCD. In fact, it is her wisdom that has helped me overcome the discouragement I've faced at times in writing this book, simply because she has such a superb understanding of how I'm wired. (For the record, she does a way better job helping me than I do helping her.)

Our Struggle Makes Us Humble and Causes Us to Rely on God

I am prone to pride. I have often thought that because I struggle with OCD, no one else has a clue what I am going through. I sometimes struggle with feeling superior in the sense that I have overcome more than others have. Because I have learned to overcome so many symptoms of my OCD, I catch myself thinking of other Christians, *"If only they would just stop complaining and being fearful, their lives would be so much better off!"*

It's funny how much the flesh craves attention, credit, and superiority. Even in my brokenness and trials, my flesh is tempted to exalt itself via the fact that I may struggle more than others.

After years of struggles such as the inability to process my thoughts, being fearful of losing my salvation, and doubting my ability to walk with God, I realize I am in no greater position than anyone else. With OCD, I can go from confidence in God to complete and utter fear that He will abandon me or that I will somehow cause Him to leave me. But thank God that He is patient with me just like a shepherd is with his wayward sheep. My many years of struggling with OCD have taught me that His love and patience aren't conditional. This has helped me understand other people's weaknesses.

This concept of pride is nothing new. In the Bible, we see examples of how God kept His people humble and reliant on Him. Apostle Paul was given amazing revelations, ones that would potentially make him prideful. He writes:

> *And lest I should be exalted above measure by the abundance of the revelations, a thorn in the flesh was given to me, a messenger of Satan to buffet me, lest I be exalted above measure. Concerning this thing I pleaded with the Lord three times that it might depart from me. And He said to me, "My grace is sufficient for you, for My strength is made perfect in weakness." Therefore most gladly I will rather boast in my infirmities, that the power of Christ*

> *may rest upon me. Therefore I take pleasure in infirmities, in reproaches, in needs, in persecutions, in distresses, for Christ's sake. For when I am weak, then I am strong.*
>
> —2 Corinthians 12:7–10

My wife dislikes the use of the word *sufficient* in this passage. She often says, "Why can't God's grace be overabundant? Why is it only sufficient?" This reminds me of the manna that Israel was given in the wilderness. God wanted them to rely on Him so much that the manna would spoil if they attempted to store it up. God does not want us to be so self-reliant that we believe the lie that we don't need Him. He can reveal Himself to us, love us, transform us, and use us most when we are close to Him, trusting Him, and relying on Him. Therefore, although it is difficult, we should thank God for the ways OCD has made us readily moldable by His hands. In fact, OCD puts us in a perfect posture to seek and receive His love. We can exalt in the fact that the result of our trials will be hope:

> *And not only that, but we also glory in tribulations, knowing that tribulation produces perseverance; and perseverance, character; and character, hope. Now hope does not disappoint, because the love of God has been poured out in our hearts by the Holy Spirit who was given to us.*
>
> —Romans 5:3–5

I attest to experiencing these Scriptures in my own life. Through the years I have looked back and seen how much God has brought me through and how much stronger I am because He allowed me to rely on His sufficient grace. Through OCD,

God has trained me to trust in Him. When days, weeks, and even months went by without relief from my mental torment, God's faithfulness was the only thing I could cling to. That has greatly strengthened me over time and helped me to remain calm when I can't figure everything out on my own. He has given me a better understanding of His glory, His goodness, and His faithfulness. Without these trials, I am confident my understanding of God would not be as deep as it is today.

The Examples of Joseph and Daniel's Friends

The story of Joseph spans several chapters in the Bible (Genesis 37, 39–50). Not knowing how his story would end, Joseph could have lost his faith, become bitter and sorry for himself, and despaired at his lot in life. But he trusted in God and ultimately saw that his pain and many trials led to the preservation of life. In everything, Joseph knew God was ultimately in control and that whatever God allowed would be for His glory. In the end, Joseph says something that shows his understanding of how God works:

> *But as for you, you meant evil against me; but God meant it for good, in order to bring it about as it is this day, to save many people alive. Now therefore, do not be afraid; I will provide for you and your little ones." And he comforted them and spoke kindly to them.*
>
> —Genesis 50:20–21

And yes, I know it seems easy for Joseph to say that God meant it for good. After all, he ended up in a very high position and became a hero in the middle of a famine. He is looking back and seeing a positive outcome. For us, we may still be in Joseph's prison, wondering if we will ever get out.

If we are, we should remember the example of Daniel's friends when they were facing death for not bowing down to the image that Nebuchadnezzar had built.

> *"If it be so, our God whom we serve is able to deliver us from the furnace of blazing fire; and He will deliver us out of your hand, O king. But even if He does not, let it be known to you, O king, that we are not going to serve your gods or worship the golden image that you have set up."*
>
> —Daniel 3:17–18

Daniel's friends chose to have faith in God, whether or not they were delivered from death. They remained faithful to God, trusting in His goodness, no matter the outcome. What an example!

If there is anything we can learn from these two stories, it is that we are to believe that God is in control. Whatever He does and allows will ultimately be used for good and is better than any plan we could devise. God has His plan for our lives.

Perspective Changes Our Conclusions

My hope is that this chapter changes your outlook, despite crushing mental challenges. Indeed, perspective matters.

> If one looks closely at any one section of Monet's paintings, we can see that each of his brush strokes provides important, discrete information: unique color, hue, texture, size and directionality, all interacting in a novel way. These component bits of information work in concert to create an image or picture on canvas. While each individual piece of information is interesting in its own right, it isn't until we step back and look at the canvas in its entirety that the masterpiece is revealed.[4]

Monet's paintings may seem downright ugly when we look at them up close. Certain parts are blotchy and unattractive to the naked eye. However, when we look from afar, in the context of the entire painting, the parts that seemed to be unattractive are actually composed of elements that contribute to the overall beauty of the painting. This is a metaphor for the earthly, temporal perspective versus the eternal one.

And so it is with OCD—and any struggle involving pain for that matter. When we focus on the amount of energy a trial has taken from us and the pain we have experienced, we can only see it as bad. When we look at how it has complicated our lives, friendships, ability to work, and perform daily functions, it seems pointless. We can be angry and unsure of God's motives.

If we are able to have God's view of us and our situation, we, like the person stepping back to admire a Monet painting, will see the purpose of our suffering. God does not always let us see, but He does ask us to always trust. Ask Him to help you trust Him more, to see His beauty and faithfulness, and to help you in the midst of your struggles.

PART II

OCD EFFECTS AND METHODS OF RESISTANCE

CHAPTER 4

LOGIC SOLVERS AND FAITH

Trying to outthink OCD has never been, and likely never will be, a common method of overcoming this disorder. However, I feel that there is a place for logical thinking in the battle against OCD. We must realize we don't have to get everything right before moving forward. I am not referring to an attempt to outsmart every thought, as that would clearly go against what research has shown is most effective. Rather, I am trying to employ a single line of logic that has led me to freedom time and time again as a means to challenge and defeat persistent and repetitive OCD thought patterns. I've studied math, finance, engineering, and actuarial science—all of which require the use of logic to solve problems. I am applying some of the approaches I learned in those contexts to my thought life. I call this methodology "logic solvers," and will demonstrate its use in the following chapter.

Weighing the 99.99% versus the .01%

As OCD sufferers, it's imperative that we examine the motives behind acquiescing to our compulsions. Are we more motivated by the desire to rid ourselves of the obsessive thought about the act or to avoid the dire consequences we fear? For example, let's look at the scenario of someone returning home to repeatedly recheck their door locks. Let's assume that after leaving for work, the person returned home five times to make sure the front door was locked. All five times it was locked, yet the person felt a very strong need to go back and check a sixth time. Instead of going back yet again, what would this person do if offered $1 million to simply say whether or not the door was actually locked? All the person would have to do is say the door was locked (after all, they had checked five times already!) and they'd get $1 million. How many of us in this scenario would say that the door was *not* locked? I'm assuming none of us. The person might have increased anxiety while they bet on the fact that the door was locked, but in the end, they would almost certainly choose to confirm that it was locked. Of course, there is a .01% chance that the door was left unlocked somehow despite five checks, but they would never bet $1 million dollars against the 99.99% chance that it was locked all along. If you agree with this line of thinking, know this: You have the ability to decipher between what you know *is true* and what you are allowing yourself to *feel might be true*!

"So what?" you might ask. Well, let's assume you let yourself bet on the door being unlocked. You would have lost out on $1 million. Therefore, by acting on your compulsive fear of the .01% chance of an event occurring, you would have ruined your chance of reaping the benefits of something you knew with 99.99% certainty was true.

And this leads to a much more important and relevant question: Are there some things we do to assuage our fear of the .01% possibility of something happening even though they have a 99.99% chance of working exactly against us?

My answer is yes! Your initial reaction might be to throw this book away right now and never read another word of it. You may be thinking, *"You don't understand! Now you've just added one more thing my mind will use to wreak havoc on me."* I can empathize with that, but I must say that this way of thinking has led to so much victory in my life that I would feel like I did a disservice to those reading this if I did not include it.

There's a way to apply logic solvers, and there are ways not to. Let's quickly review my Michael Jordan photo example from Chapter 1. When I went to a Washington Wizards game with a coworker, I got a great picture of Michael Jordan by moving down to the more expensive seats as the game was nearing its end. I later became convinced that I had stolen from the arena by sneaking to lower and more expensive seats. I was also overwhelmed by the idea that supporting a team with a wizard mascot made me a supporter of wizardry and witchcraft. Five weeks later, I had convinced myself that I could be under demonic influence. After all, I concluded, I was supporting a team whose mascot was somehow tied to witchcraft. And if this were the case, then all my thoughts had the chance of being incorrect, as I was potentially being deceived by Satan or his demons.

So, as any good OCD sufferer would do, I made an action plan that I hoped would relieve me of my fears. First, I would call Ticketmaster and pay the difference in the price between the seat I paid for and the seat I moved to. Second, I would destroy the negatives of the film as well as the pictures to prove to myself I did not treasure evil things (after all, Michael Jordan was wearing a Wizards' jersey). Last, I would reread all the Scripture I had read from the time of the game until that moment, for fear that I had read the verses with a spirit of rebellion against God and under a potential deceiving influence.

However, I did not complete my action plan. As a result, I felt overwhelmingly unworthy of praying to God, for how could I pray while being under such deception? I became convinced it was a sin for me to pray to God because I had neither "repented" nor destroyed the photo. Without repenting and performing my arduous list of duties to be make things "right," how could I think I had the ability to pray and seek God?

At this time, I realized I was in extremely dangerous territory. Stripped of the ability to pray, read the Bible, or reasonably feel that any thought I had was correct, I felt insane. This was rock bottom.

As I reflect on this time in my life, I am grateful to God for showing me a way out. The key, for me, was in recognizing that my fears—of participating in, promoting, or being influenced by evil—were all just *possibilities*. These fears were not inevitabilities, but *very low probability possibilities*. The hallmark of this disorder is the obsessive need to perform compulsions on the .01% chance that our fears might manifest themselves.

More specifically, let's look at the list of things I decided I should do in order to be made right with God. Again, if I had examined my action plan closely and with a calmer mind, I would have admitted to myself that everything I planned to do to be made right with God was done *just in case* I had erred. I would be acting based on the underlying assumption that there was no harm in performing my compulsions and that my actions could only help cover for the .01% chance that I had sinned. This is the lie that leads to bondage. Acting out on our compulsions *is* hurtful to us because it makes our relationship with God seem more about our works than about His grace. It takes what only God can give—ultimate peace, joy, and rest through His grace—and places the burden of responsibility on us to absolve our sins through our own strength.

I will break this down further in order to identify how compulsions replace God's grace with human works. My action plan was based on the underlying lie that my actions could right my sins whereas Scripture clearly states:

- *"Take My yoke upon you and learn from Me, for I am gentle and humble in heart, and you will find rest for your souls. For My yoke is easy and My burden is light"* (Matthew 11:29–30).
- *"For this is the love of God, that we keep His commandments; and His commandments are not burdensome"* (1 John 5:3).
- *"Above all, taking the shield of faith with which you will be able to quench all the fiery darts of the wicked one"* (Ephesians 6:16).

Let's look at the first verse. Was I trusting in God to be gentle and humble, and someone who would give me rest for my soul? Or was I making God's ability to give me grace conditional on my performance of a list of things I had made up? Although it seemed like rereading the Bible and destroying the pictures could cover me "just in case," I realized how damaging these rituals would be if I gave in to them. It was not that I could lose my salvation by acting out on my compulsions, but I certainly could damage my view of God and the very essence of how He wants me to view Him and in turn, respond to Him.

Ironically, my initial fear was the .01% chance that evil had somehow influenced me and hindered my ability to see God correctly. In the end, however, I realized that doing the compulsions *just in case* was the real threat to seeing Him correctly. The compulsions demanded that I appease a strict, unforgiving God who would not allow me to fellowship with Him if my performance was not perfect. Matthew 11:29–30 is the type of promise that we must use to renew our minds when we feel tempted to temporarily free ourselves from an obsessive-compulsive thought. We may remove the anxiety of the .01% chance of something terrible happening, but I propose that we are then 99.99% sure of diminishing our view of God.

Next, 1 John 5:3 showed me that Christ's commandments are not burdensome. We need to realize that our works or action plans are not prescribed in God's Word as an answer to our sins. The more I contemplated my action plan, the more I despised these false works. I knew deep down that God did not ask me to appease Him through random acts.

Finally, Ephesians 6:16 was the most crucial for me. In light of what I knew of God's Word, was I going to let myself give in to works that had nothing to do with His Word? My action plan was not based on my view of a gentle and merciful Savior or relying on God's heart to transform my own to desire to follow His commandments. The challenge in Ephesians was clear: Was I going to, *by faith,* fight against what I knew to be false, despite intense feelings pressing me to act on my compulsions just one more time?

These verses, and the logic behind their application, have helped me overcome the most intense obsessive-compulsive thoughts I've ever had. *All that is needed is a realization that going through with the compulsion is not without risk. When we realize that, we can start comparing our two options (act on the compulsion, or not) much more reasonably.*

Had I gone through with my action plan to make sure I wasn't being deceived by evil, I would have been relying on my own works to absolve my sins and make it possible for me to again understand God's Word. Of course, this would have been followed by countless additional obsessions and compulsions. Had I reread all the verses or just most of them? Was I paying perfect attention when I reread them, or would I need to re-reread them?

Rather, God's desire was to show me the truth of His Word through the Holy Spirit. Relying on myself would have been an action based on erroneous thinking—that I alone could right what I thought I had done wrong and that through my works, God would make me right with Him again.

To put it another way, as Christians with OCD, we often feel overwhelmed with the fear that we are not in God's will. We sometimes don't struggle with whether God is good or real, but rather, whether we are doing the right things to remain in good standing with Him. By using logic solvers, we are first admitting that we aren't quite sure what to do to make things right with God—that is, we are admitting that there is a possibility our compulsions are wrong and that the decision to act on our compulsions carries inherent risk. When we can admit that we don't know for sure which action to take, we can then place the responsibility to guide us on God, rather than placing ultimate responsibility on ourselves. We can change our mindset from, "*I am in sin and bear the full weight of responsibility to fix this*" to "*I'm not sure what to do, so I will lean on my gentle and faithful God to guide me and give me wisdom.*"

In my situation, I was able to admit to myself that I didn't know God's will for certain. I was faced with a choice: Should I give in to the compulsion to execute the action plan I invented to exonerate my sins, or should I ignore my urges and make the conscious choice to live by faith and trust what the Bible said, recognizing that my action plan was a list of manmade works that I should ignore? As I made the decision to admit I was unsure of which path was God's will, I was able again to pray and to remove the guilt and burden of responsibility from the process because I genuinely didn't know what to do.

Faith or Works?

As OCD sufferers, when we fall into sin or convince ourselves we have sinned, our automatic reflex is to develop a new action plan to compensate for our errors. We apply considerable creativity to the task of righting ourselves with God—i.e., correcting our errors. We might give in to the compulsion to wash our hands or read the Bible for an exact amount of time or be polite to X number of people over X number of days, and so forth. What we forget in all this activity is that God has created the ultimate "action plan" to remove the debt of sin. We are not the only people who have tried to use works to absolve our sins. We, like the Galatians, must remember Galatians 3:1–8:

> *O foolish Galatians! Who has bewitched you that you should not obey the truth, before whose eyes Jesus Christ was clearly portrayed among you as crucified? This only I want to learn from you: Did you receive the Spirit by the works of the law, or by the hearing of* ***faith****? Are you so foolish? Having begun in the Spirit, are you now being made perfect by the flesh? Have you suffered so many things in vain—if indeed it was in vain?*
>
> *Therefore He who supplies the Spirit to you and works miracles among you, does He do it by the works of the law, or by the hearing of* ***faith****?—just as Abraham "***believed*** *God, and it was accounted to him for righteousness." Therefore know that only those who are of* ***faith*** *are sons of Abraham. And the Scripture, foreseeing that God would justify the Gentiles by* faith, *preached the gospel to Abraham beforehand, saying, "In you all the nations shall be blessed."*
>
> —Galatians 3:1–8 (emphasis added)

It is abundantly clear that this passage is speaking directly to people struggling with doing works to justify themselves before God and in their own minds. When we let OCD control us, we are trying to be perfected by works, acting as the Galatians did. Did God ever ask believers to pay for their wrongs? No! If we could, then there would have been no need for a Savior. This is just as true after becoming a Christian. Our standing with God is not based on works! The same grace that saved us is the grace that keeps us from condemnation and punishment while we learn (and fail) to be more like God.

Therefore, when your compulsions are strengthening your *flesh* and crying out to be obeyed, you must learn to fight flesh with truth.

> *But that* ***no one is justified by the law*** *in the sight of God is evident, for "****the just shall live by faith.****"*
>
> —Galatians 3:11 (emphasis added)

Do you see now how vital it is not to trust in your compulsive behaviors? The question is no longer, "What if I don't do the compulsion?" Rather, the question becomes, "What if I do perform the compulsion?"

I am suggesting that if you do perform the compulsions, you are allowing yourself to fall into the trap of being made right with God through works rather than faith. Again, I cannot emphasize this enough: I am *not* referring to your *status* as a child of God, but rather how you *relate* to God as His child. This is the main concern I have for us as believers struggling with OCD—that we would let ourselves live in the power of ourselves through works, rather than in the power of God through faith. Yes, we will all be in heaven one day worshiping God together, but why not understand His goodness while on earth by overcoming compulsions with truth?

Remind yourself daily that none of your works or habitual methods of calming yourself has any power to pardon sins or gain God's favor. Moreover, they cannot calm you with any permanence. *We are saved by faith, and we walk by faith. This is where safety is found*; this is where ultimate rest lies. Charles Spurgeon addressed a similar issue:

> We will live our lives without that great risk that otherwise holds us in peril. A person runs a great risk when he steers himself. Rocks or no rocks, the peril lies in the helmsman. However, the believer is no longer the helmsman of his own vessel; he has taken a Pilot on board. To believe in God and do what He commands is a great escape from the hazards of personal weakness and folly. . . . Failure itself would be success as long as we did not fail to obey. . . . To be successful servants is not in our power, and we will not be held responsible for it. *Our greatest risk is over when we obey. God makes faith and obedience the way of safety.* (emphasis added)[1]

What encouraging words! "Our greatest risk is over when we obey." And what is obedience for us with OCD? To ignore our compulsions to "do, do, and do some more," and simply live our lives knowing we are right with God by faith and *not* by some torturous ritual we have conceived for ourselves. Additionally, Spurgeon writes:

> Especially in the old days, it was believed that misery and merit went together, so men tortured themselves so that they MIGHT please God. They went for many days without washing themselves or their clothes; they mistakenly believed that, in this way, they acquired

the odor of sanctity. I do not believe that Jesus thinks any person is any more His friend because he is dirty.

Some put on hair shirts, which made raw wounds. I do not think the kindly Lord Jesus counts this as a friendly act. Ask any humane person whether he would be gratified by knowing that a friend wore a hair shirt for his sake, and he would answer, "Please let the poor creature wear whatever is most comfortable for him, and that will please me best."

The loving Jesus does not take delight in pain and discomfort; forcing one's body to waste away is no doctrine of His. John the Baptist might have been an ascetic, but certainly Jesus was not. He came "eating and drinking" (Matt. 11:19), a man among men. He did not come to demand the rigors of a hermitage or a monastery, or else He never would have been seen at feasts. When we hear of the nuns of St. Ann sleeping bolt upright in their coffins, we take no particular satisfaction in their doing so; a kind heart would beg them to go to bed.[2]

Anything that is not commanded in Scripture is superstition.[3]

Fear of Sin and Misconceptions of Repentance

As OCD sufferers, we carry a heavy burden of dread and guilt because we live in constant fear that we might be sinning. We can spend nearly all our time worrying about the .01% chance we are in sin (e.g., thinking, *"Oh no, I may have accidentally offended that acquaintance by smiling at them the wrong way"*). I have found it amazingly helpful to rely on my ability to consciously recognize the compulsive act that my OCD insists will temporarily free me from this fear (e.g., finding the acquaintance and awkwardly apologizing). After the realization is acknowledged consciously, I can claim the promise in James 1:5: *"If any of you lacks wisdom, let him ask of God, who gives to all generously and without reproach, and it will be given to him."*

This verse is freeing because it clearly shows not only that we can pray to God for wisdom in these situations, but also that we are commanded to! By consciously applying logic to our thought life and recognizing that while we think we may be in sin, we are fundamentally unsure, and we can recognize the need to seek clarity from our all-knowing Father. By moving through these steps, we extricate ourselves from obsessive thinking about our guilt and refocus our minds on our God, His power, and His wisdom. With my mind refocused in this way, I have found that more often than not, I end up forgetting about the original potential sin altogether because I was not in sin in the first place!

However, some of you might still ask, "What about repentance? If I have sinned, isn't there something I should do to be made right with God? It sounds like you're saying we should never do anything to change no matter how convinced we are that we did something wrong."

It is critical that OCD sufferers understand the answer to this question for two reasons. First, we need to understand what God expects of us in terms of repentance. Second, we need to grasp just how awesome the grace of God is toward us.

Restitution versus True Repentance

As OCD sufferers, we must internalize this fundamental truth: We are no longer slaves to sin. We have been set free through the blood of Jesus. We must break free from the thought patterns that convince us that we still need to be punished daily for our sins and that we must "pay" for our wrongdoings. For many of us, it is easy to fall into the trap of believing that our guilt and our compulsions are an outpouring of repentance. The problem is that this is not true repentance!

For example, let's assume a man regularly steals from a 7-Eleven store. Afterward, he would feel terribly guilty, so he would give some of what he stole to the poor to rid himself of the guilt. However, he never had the intention of not stealing again. He only gave to make himself feel better. So, he performed this ritual over and over again.

That is the trap many of us fall into—the trap of restitution. We are not repenting when we do something out of a compulsive motive to ease an emotion (often guilt) or to pay a debt for what is owed due to a sin. This, by definition, is *restitution*. True repentance (*metanoia* in Greek) means a reversal of a decision.[4] In other words, the man who stole from 7-Eleven would be repenting if he made a final decision to stop stealing from 7-Eleven. The act of giving to the poor to ease his own guilt and to somehow even the scales of his "right-doing" versus his wrongdoing would have nothing to do with true repentance. Repentance is a simple decision to not do something anymore. And unlike earthly authorities who require restitution for wrongs, God does not require any payment for our sins because Christ has paid it all!

Faith Is Relying on God, Not Our Compulsions

Luke 7 provides us with a tremendous example of what our God desires most from us. In the story of the woman with the perfume, we see that God does not desire perfect people. Simon saw the woman "who was a sinner" and her actions from the perspective of the world. He viewed her sin with contempt—a sinner unworthy to touch a prophet of God. Jesus viewed her through His lens as a loving Father, desiring only her repentance and her love. Her gift offering, her emotion, and her actions were the physical outpouring of a repentant and loving heart.

And behold, a woman in the city who was a sinner, when she knew that Jesus sat at the table in the Pharisee's house, brought an alabaster flask of fragrant oil, and stood at His feet behind Him weeping; and she began to wash His feet with her tears, and wiped them with the hair of her head; and she kissed His feet and anointed them with the fragrant oil. Now when the Pharisee who had invited Him saw this, he spoke to himself, saying, "This Man, if He were a prophet, would know who and what manner of woman this is who is touching Him, for she is a sinner."

And Jesus answered and said to him, "Simon, I have something to say to you."

So he said, "Teacher, say it."

"There was a certain creditor who had two debtors. One owed five hundred denarii, and the other fifty. And when they had nothing with which to repay, he freely forgave them both. Tell Me, therefore, which of them will love him more?"

Simon answered and said, "I suppose the one whom he forgave more."

And He said to him, "You have rightly judged." Then He turned to the woman and said to Simon, "Do you see this woman? I entered your house; you gave Me no water for My feet, but she has washed My feet with her tears and wiped them with the hair of her head You gave Me no kiss, but this woman has not ceased to kiss My feet since the time I came in. You did not anoint My head with oil, but this woman has anointed My feet with fragrant oil.

> *Therefore I say to you, her sins, which are many, are forgiven, for she loved much. But to whom little is forgiven, the same loves little."*
>
> *Then He said to her, "Your sins are forgiven."*
>
> —Luke 7:37–48

Do you see how amazing Christ is—how revolutionary his approach to "religion" must have been in the eyes of the Pharisee? The woman's sins were many, but she offered Jesus no penance, no restitution. Yet, Jesus said, "Your sins have been forgiven" and praised her in the presence of a highly religious man. The woman knew there was nothing she could do to erase her sins, cleanse herself, or gain God's forgiveness, so she fell at Jesus's feet in repentance. The image is powerful, and the contrast between her, weeping on the ground, and the Pharisee, sitting in judgment at the table, is compelling. God desires a heart that is compelled by repentance and love, not a mind obsessively focused on perfect or "religious" behavior. God asks that we focus on His goodness, not our own abilities to perform.

When challenged by overwhelming compulsions, remember the position of the woman at Jesus's feet and know that your heart's desire to love and please God is the most worthy sacrifice. There is no need to worry about the .01% chance that we may be sinning. God leads us with great care and attention. We are His sheep, and He will leave the 99 to go find the one that has strayed. Sheep by their very nature are stupid and tend to wander, so even if our intentions lead us into potentially dangerous situations, God is right there interceding for us and guiding us. Remember Philippians 1:6, which says that *"He who has begun a good work in you will complete it until the day of Jesus Christ."* This is the kind of God we serve, and we should live out our faith in Him by relying on Him rather than our compulsions.

Discerning God's Will

Another outcropping of OCD sufferers' fear of sinning reveals itself in anxiety over God's will. As OCD sufferers, we are plagued by the fear, "What if it's not God's will?" or "What if I make this minor decision incorrectly? How will it affect the future?" We all too commonly continue in this line of thinking so far as to conclude that one decision could adversely impact our friends, family, communities, and even the entire universe. This level of fear can affect us so severely that even simple decisions such as where to eat, what video game to play, or when to do laundry can be totally immobilizing. We get stuck thinking that we might make an irreversibly wrong decision that could have catastrophic consequences. Thus, decision-making is a tortuous process that often leaves us paralyzed. In our exhaustion and panic, we conclude that we can't decipher between what is and isn't God's will.

In my case, this was a major roadblock when trying to make many small decisions in the past. For example, in college I had several places on campus to go for dinner. I often wondered if I could potentially offset God's plan for my life if I went to a dining location that He did not intend for me. Or even worse, I wondered that if I went to the "wrong" place, I would bump into the "wrong" people and somehow derail their lives from God's will for them.

In order to correct this line of thinking, we have to recognize that it is not our ability to make good decisions that we need to examine, but rather it is our view of God that needs examining. Again, we must use logic to recognize that our view of God leads us to fear the potential negative consequences of a decision. In other words, this hurdle has nothing to do with our lack of discernment in how to make right choices, but rather our view of God. And what does the Word of God tell us about Him? That He is all-knowing; He is a good and loving Father; He is our Advocate, and more. Knowing this, should we abide in fear that He will let us make a negative life-changing decision on a whim? No!

I want you to know that you can lean on the character of God to overcome the crippling fear of decision-making. It is a step of faith to rest in the knowledge of God's goodness and kindness. In so doing, we will find freedom from the fear of making mistakes. We won't be able to figure out every single thing we should ever do, but we can focus on the true character of God whenever confronted with a decision. When our view of God is corrected, our fear of being outside His will is also corrected. Rest in the assurance in Romans 8:34: "*Who is he who condemns? It is Christ who died, and furthermore is also risen, who is even at the right hand of God, who also makes intercession for us.*"

Doubting by Habit

Because of OCD, we oftentimes have the tendency to question things so much that we even question the obvious. The hurdle isn't uncertainty of God's will; it's more that we doubt everything by habit.

As with most things, the Bible is very helpful when it comes to deciphering God's will. God uses His Word, circumstances, others' encouragement, and the peace of His Holy Spirit to confirm His will. As OCD sufferers, we can often see that our desires are in line with the Word of God and that circumstances have allowed us to pursue our desires. Yet we are often stuck wondering why we don't have God's peace. So, we remain frozen, not pursuing the very things our hearts desire.

This happened to me when I was in college. I was a photographer for the school newspaper, and our football team had just landed one of the most talented football players in history. I wanted so badly to take pictures at a game and was finally given a chance. It was thrilling to be on the sidelines right where the action was, with tens of thousands of screaming fans behind me.

A few days after the event, the photo editor came to me and told me I did a great job, and that I should "consider" shooting more games. "Consider!" The suggestion was an honor, and I was trying not to tear up from joy as I walked away from the conversation. My logical self knew there was nothing to consider! This was an opportunity of a lifetime. However, within moments my OCD kicked into high gear. I immediately began feeling guilty and thought to myself, *"Maybe I shouldn't pursue this. After all, I might get prideful and fall away from God."*

With thoughts like this hounding us at the most thrilling times of our lives, it's no wonder we struggle to sense the peace of God; we're too busy condemning ourselves! Let's take a moment to examine this example to evaluate my fear using the 99.99% versus the .01% principle. What was the proof that there was a 99.99% chance that I was in God's will?

- I was seeking to know God's will and genuinely wanting to know what He wanted me to do.
- God had given me the talent to take good enough pictures that the editor wanted me at more football games.
- I had a very strong desire to do photography. This was a joy to me, even though it involved a huge time commitment and lugging around pounds of equipment for hours on end.
- Christians close to me continually said I had a talent and that I should pursue photography.

Frankly, there was no reason at all for me to doubt that the opportunity was an incredible gift from God—a gift that was personal, given based on His knowledge of me and my gifts and my delights, intended to bring me joy. But I almost let it slide away because there was a .01% chance it wasn't God's will. If I chose to believe that the opportunity was not God's will, I would also be turning away from acknowledging how good God was to me in that moment.

In order to evaluate the situation, I flipped the scenario on its head. This helped me see the error in my logic. I came to realize that if I did not love photography, I would not have hesitated to take the opportunity. I would have thought, *"Surely, God has given me this opportunity. I have no desire to do it, but I should take this God-given opportunity. No worries here; no matter how hard I work at it, this will never become an idol."* How horrible! If I had walked away from the gift that God gave me, I would have been acting out on underlying doubts in His goodness.

And this is where we must apply logic solvers. The chance of being *out* of God's will by not further pursuing football photography was higher than the risk of taking the opportunity. If I took the opportunity, there was the .01% chance I would make it an idol, but I was unsure if this would even happen. If I did not take the opportunity, there was a 99.99% chance I would be acting on the belief, doubt, or fear that God was not good and that He didn't want me to enjoy the gifts He had given me. I was almost sure I would miss out on relishing in God's goodness to me. Logically, there was a greater threat of drawing away from God if I acted on the belief that He was not good than if I acted in faith and acknowledgement of his goodness.

Another common pitfall for OCD sufferers is allowing OCD's treatment of us (the condemning, demanding, and terrifying thought patterns within us) to impact how we view God's treatment of us. God's view of us could not be more opposite than OCD's! Our God is full of mercy, kindness, love, and patience. He is slow to anger and sets us free from bondage to sin and death. We have a

Master whose goodness can never be questioned! Our God works all we do together for good. Even if we take the abilities, time, and money He has given us and invest in activities that never amount to anything, God will be pleased with us if we faithfully believe in His character and trust that He will pick us up when we fall. Remember, if God is for us, who can be against us?

In conclusion, the truth is that we are *not* all-knowing, all-wise, sinless, or perfect at decision-making (even though we want to be). Yes, desiring holiness pleases God, but compulsive rituals that temporarily absolve our guilt or ease anxiety are not what God wants from us. Those actions do not have the power to make us more like Christ, nor does He take pleasure in seeing us suffer through these ritualized processes. Instead, God wants our deficiencies and weaknesses to point us to complete reliance on Him and His mercy, forgiveness, faithfulness, goodness, guidance, and wisdom. He is the one who redeems us from all our sins. In the end, it is God's character that sets us free. Even if we make wrong decisions, our Father can redeem us and will be faithful to save us.

CHAPTER 5

THE ROLE OF MEDICATION

Taking medication for a mental illness as well as the existence of mental illness is controversial among some Christians. This chapter will examine some biblical and theological reasoning that supports the use of medicine. However, I want to underscore that we should not attempt to replace the power of God with the use of medicine. Rather, we should take full advantage of the medical advancements God has allowed in recent decades to position ourselves to receive God's power.

I want to add that I have experienced the power of God in incredible ways at times in my life, and I know that He is able to heal our bodies and souls at His will. I believe He has the power to heal mental, spiritual, and medical conditions. He can therefore most assuredly heal us from OCD any time He chooses.

Isn't OCD Just Spiritual Warfare?

Our body, soul, and spirit affect each other; we are not comprised of just one of these entities. So, to say OCD is 100% spiritual overlooks much of what we know scientifically. In fact, scans show differences in the brains of people with OCD versus those who do not have this disorder. In many cases, low serotonin has been associated with high gamma wave activity. Attached is an image of two scans that contrast the high energy use in the brains of people with and without OCD (normal control).

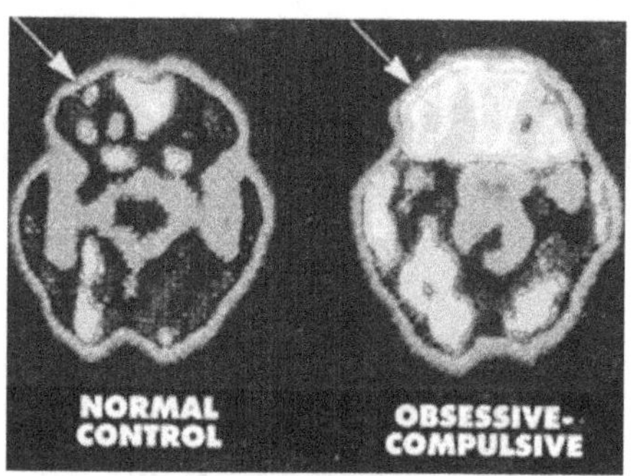

HIGH ENERGY USE IN THE BRAIN OF A TYPICAL PERSON WITH OCD[1]

Furthermore, the field of medicine recognizes OCD as a medical illness. Psychiatrist Ian Osborn, MD, writes:

> Indeed, the majority of recent scientific papers on OCD deal with the biomedical aspect of the illness. Research in this area is so impressive that the United States Congress has seen fit to include OCD among a small group of mental disorders covered by the Mental Health Equitable Treatment Act. Thus, OCD has been officially recognized as being just as "biologically based" as diabetes or heart disease, and therefore deserving of the same insurance coverage.[2]

I love that Osborn states that OCD is "as biologically based as diabetes" because both conditions are treated by changing a chemical level in the body. Diabetes is treated by introducing insulin into the blood stream to lower blood glucose levels, and some medications used to treat OCD (known as SSRIs) increase serotonin levels. In terms of morality, I find it is hard to argue that treating diabetes by reducing blood glucose with insulin is any different than treating low serotonin levels with SSRIs.

However, the way believers typically view the approach to coping with diabetes and OCD can be quite different. In high school, a diabetic girl in our youth group passed out during a sermon and was in dire need of sugar (her insulin shot had dangerously lowered her blood sugar level). Someone alerted the pastor, who immediately asked the congregation if anyone had candy or glucose pills. A few medical doctors, including my mom, rushed to assist the girl, while the pastor prayed for her recovery before proceeding with his sermon. Nobody stood up to protest the request for sugar, and I'm not aware of anyone who contacted the church leadership team to convey their disapproval. Why? Because diabetes is accepted as a medical (physical) condition by both secular society and nearly all denominations of Christianity.

However, I have met numerous people, including close family members, who clearly object to using medication to treat OCD. Even for some who understand that OCD is partially a chemical problem, the stigma surrounding the use of medicine for mental illness is difficult to overcome. I believe that this stigma is rooted in the belief that OCD is in no way a physical or medical issue and is solely spiritual. If that were not the belief, then the same Christians that advocate for the use of medicine to control diabetes would claim that diabetes should be fought only within the spiritual realm.

Isn't OCD Just Physical?

What about all the OCD thoughts that torment us regarding our safety in Christ, our eternal salvation, our ability to know God's will, and so forth? To say it's not interrelated with spiritual warfare also seems nonsensical. OCD is definitely caused at least in part by a physical ailment (a serotonin imbalance in the brain), but I also know that Satan and his demons are out to attack our minds. We have a disorder that makes us more apt to obsess about things we would otherwise not dwell on, but thoughts that challenge our faith in God's love and goodness do seem potentially spiritual in nature. My argument takes both the physical and spiritual realms into consideration in terms of developing a strategy to overcome OCD. I propose that if we address the physical part of the equation by physical means that will enable us to fight the spiritual aspect of the illness with less hindrance.

To illustrate, I use the following example. Imagine a world-class kickboxer, one of the best, with one major problem: he is incredibly closed off from the world and overly protected by his trainer. The trainer is also world-class and has one major problem: he is closed-minded about injuries. He believes a physical injury exists only if there is blood to show for it. Therefore, anytime the boxer has a busted nose, it is taken care of immediately. However, one day the boxer suffers a severely bruised rib during a bout. After the fight he describes the pain to his trainer, pleading for an X-ray. However, because no blood is visible, the trainer shrugs off the injury as whining and having a poor attitude.

In this scenario, two things would occur. First, the boxer would be extremely frustrated because he wouldn't know how to make his trainer listen. Because he is isolated from the world, he would have to trust his trainer as he always had. He may reason that the trainer was the one who got him to the top in the first place. Second, the boxer would get creamed in his future matches. All his opponents would discover his bad rib and position themselves to maximize their advantage against this weakness.

OCD sufferers are like this boxer. We are weakened in our ability to fight our intrusive thoughts due to our hidden physical injury. Our continual struggle to feel God's presence or be more obedient in an effort to overcome the illness results in futility over and over again. And this leaves us in despair. Our injury is hidden, and the lack of support from other Christians who cannot see the real physical nature of OCD can contribute to our hopelessness. To say Satan never uses these situations to his advantage is naïve in my opinion.

In *The Christian's Secret to a Happy Life*, Hannah Whitall Smith addresses what this looks like long before OCD was ever defined. Just replace the words *temptation* and *wrong* with the phrase *intrusive thoughts*, and we can see how Satan could easily use this illness to his advantage.

> It seems hardly worthwhile to say that temptation is not sin, and yet much distress arises from not understanding this fact. The very suggestion of wrong seems to bring pollution with it; and the poor tempted soul begins to feel as if it must be very bad indeed, and very far off from God, to have had such thoughts and suggestions. It is as though a burglar should break into a man's house to steal, and, when the master of the house begins to resist him and to drive him out, should turn round and accuse the owner of being himself the thief. It is the enemy's grand ruse for entrapping us. He comes and whispers suggestions of evil to us, – doubts, blasphemies, jealousies, envyings, and pride, and then turns round and says, "Oh, how wicked you must be to think of such things! It is very plain that you are not trusting the Lord; for if you had been, it would have been impossible for these things to have entered your heart." This reasoning sounds so very plausible that we often accept it as true, and so come under condemnation, and are filled with discouragement.[3]

This happens even more when OCD is left untreated outside the spiritual realm. Like the boxer, Christians with OCD are world-class citizens; they have Christ living in them and have the ability to live life abundantly. Their OCD is the equivalent of a broken rib, and the enemy takes advantage. And often, like in the case of the isolated boxer, all they hear are the views of their peers, family members, and even pastoral counselors who are blind to their physical injury. They are pushed away from medicine and told that their faith needs to be strengthened. Worse yet, they are often encouraged to repent of a sin that is causing the problem. As in the boxer's case, Christians with OCD are often severely frustrated and emotionally defeated, which is exactly where Satan wants them to be.

John Bunyan, the seventeenth-century preacher and writer, gives us an amazing picture of what this looks like. He was constantly tortured by the thought that Christ did not die for a specific sin he had committed. Here are just a few snippets from his book *Grace Abounding*, in which he faces the emotional storms of OCD as the waves of condemnation came and went:

> So, because of the strange and unusual assaults of Satan, my soul was like a broken vessel driven by the winds and tossed, sometimes headlong into despair. . . . Oh, the thought of imaginations, frights, fears, and terrors that are brought about by a thorough application of guilt combined with desperation![4]

Later, Bunyan describes crying out to God, pleading that he be shown His love. He immediately receives comfort from the verse stating, "I have loved thee with an everlasting love," goes to sleep quietly and wakes the next morning with the verse fresh in his mind. But again, he writes:

> The tempter still did not leave me alone, but must have tried to cause me to doubt God's Word at least a hundred times that day. I met with many severe attacks and conflicts as I tried to hold on to God's Word. The verse about Esau not finding repentance would fly in my face like lightning. My heart and emotions would sometimes be up and down twenty times an hour, yet God gave me strength and kept my heart upon His Word, from which I had also, for several days in a row, much sweetness and comfortable hope of pardon. It was as if God was telling me, "I loved you while you were committing this sin. I loved you before, I love you now, and I will love you forever."[5]

Bunyan is comforted by the thought that he was loved and still a friend of God. This leaves him completely in love with God, and he states, "If I had a thousand gallons of blood within my veins, I would have freely spilled it all at the command and feet of my Lord and Savior." [6]

> The word was fulfilled on me, and I was also refreshed by it, that I would be ashamed and never open your mouth anymore because of your humiliation, when I have forgiven you for all that you have done, the Lord GOD declares (Ezekiel 16:63). So my soul was at this time, and I thought it would forever be, set free from being again afflicted with my former guilt and disbelief.[7]

Sadly, Bunyan's peace and joy switches to guilt and condemnation yet again in the very next paragraph: "But before many weeks were over, I began to despond again, fearing that I might still be deceived and destroyed in the end, even after all that I had recently enjoyed."[8]

Bunyan goes on to admit that this tormenting cycle lasted for years:

> Indeed it was, for I found no deliverance or peace for nearly two and a half years. Those words, though in themselves they tended to discouragement, yet to me, who was afraid that this condition would be eternal, were sometimes helpful and refreshing to me, as they gave me hope that the assault would end at last.[9]

Bunyan continues the chapter in a similar fashion, describing the comfort of God's forgiveness, then his fear of eternal condemnation, back to comfort again, only to be met with intense condemnation once more. At one point Bunyan remembers a Bible passage about those who have great faith, which makes him earnestly pray to God:

> Yet *I was not able to believe this, that this was a prayer of faith, till almost six months after*; for I could not think that I had faith, or that there should be a word for me to act faith on; therefore I should still be, as sticking in the jaws of desperation, and went mourning up and down in a sad condition. (emphasis added)[10]

For Bunyan, the battles continued relentlessly:

> By these words I was sustained for about seven or eight weeks, yet not without many conflicts. My peace would come and go, sometimes twenty times

> a day; first comfort, then trouble; peace would come, but before I could walk a quarter mile, I would be as full of fear and guilt as ever any heart could hold. This did not just happen occasionally, but it happened the entire seven or eight weeks. Like a pair of scales in my mind, my thoughts would race back and forth. Sometimes the sufficiency of grace would be uppermost, and other times the thought of Esau's parting with his birthright would reign, depending upon whether I was in peace or turmoil.[11]

What begins as a physical issue in the brain can be used by the enemy to attack our hearts. Accepting the truth that some mental disorders are medically treatable and then treating them as such will help those with OCD fight their spiritual battles and bring healing and relief to so many.

When an intrusive thought crosses an OCD sufferer's mind, I don't think we can know whether it is specifically the disorder or whether Satan is spiritually attacking us by way of our OCD thoughts. However, I am confident that without OCD, Bunyan would never have had to say, "My peace would be in it, and out, sometimes 20 times a day" or admit to emotional defeat within weeks of strong victory or acknowledge that he had no peace for 30 months straight. What we know for sure is that Satan is out to kill, steal, and destroy as John 10:10 declares. I am convinced by my own personal experience that I am best armed to combat Satan's lies when I first treat the physical aspects of OCD via medicine or other means, which include sleep and exercise. This is something I've learned over the years, to the point where if I start to feel spiritually attacked in a way similar to how OCD attacks, my first thought is not that I need to fast or pray but to exercise more consistently (which is also believed to increase serotonin levels).

Does Taking Medicine Take Away God's Glory?

One of the main purposes of the Christian life is to glorify God. Which begs the question: Do we limit God's ability to be glorified in us by taking medication for OCD? Only faith in Christ raises people from spiritual death, and only God gets the glory for the gift of salvation and a spirit alive in Christ. God and God alone can forgive the sins of man, and for that He receives all the glory. This is clearly seen in Matthew 9:4–6, when Christ asks the Pharisees (who were accusing Him of blasphemy in their hearts):

> *"Why do you think evil in your hearts? For which is easier, to say, 'Your sins are forgiven you,' or to say, 'Arise and walk'? But that you may know that the Son of Man has power on earth to forgive sins" —then He said to the paralytic, "Arise, take up your bed, and go to your house."*

I am alive in Christ because of Christ alone. God receives glory when we obey His commands by faith. In the same way that a follower of Christ can wear a cast on his broken arm and be obedient to God (or undergo chemotherapy to fight cancer or ingest medication to control cholesterol), we can take medication for mental illness and be obedient to God.

The Vital Difference between a Trial and the Testing of One's Faith

I feel that some Christians ask us to stay in bondage to OCD because they define OCD as a trial God put in our path, and they think that removing it would be outside His plan for our lives. This is where a very important distinction must be made between a trial and the testing of our faith. James 1:2–4 says, *"My brethren, count it all joy when you fall into various **trials**, knowing that the **testing of your faith** produces **patience**. But let patience have its **perfect work**, that you may be perfect and complete, lacking nothing"* (emphasis added). This passage clearly commands us to let patience have its perfect work. And what produces patience? The testing of our faith. The trials are in the temporal world, but the more significant battleground for the believer is in the spiritual realm where our faith is tested, and patience has its perfect work in us.

There is no command to stay in a trial if a non-sinful path out of it is available. Also, nowhere in the Bible does God ask us to stay in a trial when freedom can be found (without sinning against God). So, why don't we *see OCD as the trial, and the temptation to stop believing in God's goodness as the testing of our faith?* When we do so, we will be much more inclined to get help from Christian counselors and possibly even medication to diminish the strength of the disorder, knowing that our battleground is in the spiritual and not the temporal world. When we let go of the idea that the disorder is what produces the "perfect work" in us and that our calling is to endure OCD (even though we have options to escape this trial), we can seek practical methods to find freedom from the disorder. Freedom means we can focus our beleaguered minds on what matters—namely, allowing patience to have its perfect work in us by fighting the good fight of faith and holding onto the promise of God's goodness despite the trials that come and go in this life.

We don't need to cling to any particular trial to refine us; we simply need to cling to God to refine us—that is faith and patience in action. If he provides us with opportunities to find healing for physical limitations, there is no reason to hesitate. In fact, Christian counselors and doctors can be used by God to reveal more powerful lessons to us about God's goodness and how He works through feeble people to accomplish His will. Through others we might learn that God is for us and can bring us relief and victory. While God is glorified in the midst of—and through—our suffering, His glory is not born of our suffering. Therefore, there is no need to remain in a state of pain to ensure that God is glorified.

God Is Always Doing the Healing

Let's examine what actually happens when a doctor treats a broken limb. Please note that the doctor *treats* a limb; he does not *heal* the limb. When a broken bone is set, the body actually does the healing. The doctor only gets credit for what he was trained to do, while God gets the glory (indirectly) for making the body so amazing that it can heal itself. A doctor can set a bone, but the body (God's creation) makes it heal—much in the same way that Paul states, *"I planted, Apollos watered, but God gave the increase. So then neither he who plants is anything, nor he who waters, but God who gives the increase"* (1 Corinthians 3:6–7).

A relative I deeply respect once told me that it was a shame I trusted God for so long and then went on medication—as if to say God's grace had brought me so far, but then I was giving up on God and relying on medicine to do the rest. The underlying belief that makes this assessment inaccurate is the idea that medicine or doctors heal by their own power. Referring to Paul's statement above, it's like believing the farmer produces the fruits of the field by his own power. Ultimately, it is God who heals and grows, and he allows us to play a part in it. This does not take away from God's glory.

My hope is that believers will consider medication in the same way they see the setting of a broken bone: a bone is set in order to stabilize, prevent further injury, and place the body in position to heal itself and return to proper functioning. In the same way, medication helps to stabilize the mind, prevent further injury, and place the mind in a more stable position to begin healing and return to proper functioning. In both cases, God gets the glory because the body is doing what God created it to do. Christians taking medication for OCD can rest assured that medicine is not the source of power in their ultimate path to victory. Furthermore, they are not denying God the opportunity to work powerfully in their lives, nor are they demonstrating a lack of trust or reliance on Him for healing. Healing still comes by God's divine power. Would Christians ask other Christians, or even their own children, to endure the pain and potential lifelong disability caused by a broken bone instead of seeking medical attention? Would they see the setting of a broken bone as an act of faithlessness or a turning away from reliance on God's provision over their lives? Certainly not!

I encourage Christians to avoid falling into the trap of believing that denying medical intervention is somehow a more spiritual or righteous response to OCD and that their faith is proven through the denial of medication. As OCD sufferers, we must be mindful of the trap of becoming sanctimonious in our suffering and prayerfully consider options that might help us for the sake of ourselves, our Christian walk, and those around us who help bear our burdens.

How Do We View God's Provision?

As Christians we freely acknowledge that God provides. We all have seen examples of great miracles that have occurred throughout history or on the mission field or in the Church body. However, when it comes to believing that God will provide for us personally, in very practical ways, we may hesitate.

But God has always provided for His children. Soon after Adam and Eve chose to disobey God, He gave them grace by sacrificing the first animals to make skin coverings for them. During the time of Moses, the Israelites needed to learn to trust God, so He implemented a system whereby they would need to trust Him daily for their food, manna. This we rightfully see as God's intervention and provision.

However, do we fail to recognize that, despite living thousands of years later, we are still in need of daily physical sustenance? Who provides for us? Yes, we can water plants that provide food for ourselves, but who makes them grow? Who makes them bear fruit? Who provides the water and allows the sun to shine? God does! And in the midst of sickness, suffering, and death, who allowed for the invention of penicillin? God did! So, how can we acknowledge that God provided in this way and then think that God did not provide the breakthroughs in medicine for mental health disorders? Isn't God asking us to accept with gratitude the practical ways He provides help? A humorous and simple story demonstrates this point:

> I'm sure you have heard the story about the man who faced imminent danger as a result of a flood that began to ravage his community. The floodwaters rose higher, forcing him to retreat to the roof of his house. On two occasions, individuals in boats beckoned him to climb into their boats and save his life. But he refused and shouted back from his roof, "I'm a Christian! God will save me!"
>
> Finally, the waters rose to the edge of the roof. Suddenly a helicopter appeared and begged the man to grab the dropped latter [*sic*] and be saved. Well, you know what happened! The man refused and ultimately died. When he entered heaven, he demanded to see God. "Why did you let me drown?" Instead of striking him down with a lightning bolt, God calmly replied, "Hey, I sent you two boats and a helicopter."[12]

Medicine in the Bible

Hezekiah Commanded to Use Physical Treatment

Although it is not a major biblical theme, taking measures to cure physical illness is definitely addressed in the Bible. When King

Hezekiah had a boil that was threatening his health to the point of death, Isaiah the prophet came to him and said, "*Thus says the* LORD, *'Set your house in order, for you shall die and not live'*" (Isaiah 38:1).

Throughout the rest of Isaiah 38, Hezekiah seeks the restoration of his life and weeps bitterly. In the end, he is healed. However, it is very interesting to me that the chapter does not conclude with a verse saying something to the effect of "and God healed him." Rather, we see that he was given specific instructions to apply a cake of figs to his boil, "that he may recover" (Isaiah 38:21).

From this, we see that God's healing is not limited to the supernatural through our faith, but He also allows the use of physical means to heal. Notice also that faith was not removed as a component of healing.

Luke and the Practice of Medicine

Luke is called "the beloved physician" in Colossians 4:14. The use of that phrase shows that the author, Apostle Paul, clearly accepted and embraced that profession. Otherwise, he would have likely referred to him with a phrase such as "a beloved brother" and then either criticized or made no mention of Luke's vocation.

Paul Recommended Wine for Ailments

> *No longer drink only water, but use a little wine for your stomach's sake and your frequent infirmities.*
>
> —1 Timothy 5:23

Regarding what Apostle Paul meant by infirmities, he used the word *astheneia*,[13] which means feebleness (of body or mind), implying malady, moral frailty—disease, infirmity, sickness, weakness. And so, it seems that to take medicine to help with disease and sickness is not such a big leap from drinking wine, a substance neither produced by the body nor found naturally, for the very same purpose.

Finally, I want to comment on what the Bible does **not** say about using medicine for healing. It does not say that it is a sin to use medicine, that it's an idol, that using it replaces faith in God, or that we are to avoid it. There are many places in the Bible where sins are specifically listed, and none of those passages list the use of medicine.

A Common Argument against OCD Medication

Many Christians argue that those who take medicine for OCD do not have enough faith. Stating that someone is lacking faith for using medical advancements that God has allowed is akin to telling someone he is sinning for taking a spoonful of Mylanta for an upset stomach. Both indigestion and OCD are caused by a chemical imbalance we are often unaware of. In the same way you cannot renew your mind to settle your stomach, you cannot add serotonin to your brain the moment you feel the onset of OCD symptoms. In the same way that Mylanta brings the stomach's acidity down to a pain-free level, OCD medication brings serotonin levels up to a more functional level. It is important to see just how close medical and mental health treatments are in many cases.

Medication does not fight the fight of faith for you. As a Christian, part of your assignment from God is to fight the fight of faith. Much like the boxer, you must train (your mind) and put your knowledge of God's Word and character to use in your daily life.

I'm stating the obvious here in the event that you are hesitant to use medication because you are concerned that it will take away from your reliance on God. To be honest, when my relative said it was a shame that God's grace brought me so far and that I was now going to take meds, it jarred me for several days. I feared that the medicine would somehow replace my reliance on God's grace in my fight against OCD.

The key to overcoming this belief is to recognize that God's call on our life is not to fight the valiant fight for good health. Does God's Word ask us to fight the flu by faith, or to fight migraines through faith in God? Christian OCD sufferers must focus on what God asks of us through His Word regarding the fight of faith. Medicine will not do the Christian life for you. It will not fill you with the fruit of the Spirit. It will not do the work in you that God wants to do. It will not make you more Christlike.

Rather, medicine will help you heal so that you can fight the spiritual fight of faith in strength, and less disabled by injury. In *Blue Genes*, Paul Meier, MD, describes two seminary students who suffered from the same severe mental condition. They both sought counseling, but only one sought medical treatment. He went on to finish seminary and became a pastor. The other student refused treatment and declined to the point where he could no longer function in society.[14] What matters here is not each man's level of success, but the condition of each man's heart in relation to God. This example begs the question as to whether refusal to accept the gift of modern medicine is based more in fear and doubt than it is in faith in God's goodness. Are we so fearful of sinning that we fail to address our own physical ailments? Again, viewing God as merciful and full of favor toward us makes the risk of doing the "wrong thing" by taking medication a moot point.

The Difference between a Trial, Being in Bondage, and Self-Inflicted Torment

I once heard a sermon about how believers should never try to escape the trials that God puts them through. God can use trials in amazing ways for His purposes and for our blessing. In 1 Corinthians 7:20–23, Paul writes:

> *Let each one remain in the same calling in which he was called. Were you called while a slave? Do not be concerned about it;* ***but if you can be made free, rather use it.*** *For he who is called in the Lord while a slave is the Lord's freedman. Likewise he who is called while free is Christ's slave. You were bought at a price; do not become slaves of men.* (emphasis added)

In this passage, Paul asked everyone to stay in the position they were in when they came to a saving faith. Therefore, it is easy to conclude that if we are in bondage to OCD (and that is exactly what it is, bondage), then we should do nothing in our power to get out of that position.

However, please note that Paul specifically says, "but" if you are able to become free, rather do that. Never does God ask us to stay in bondage for the sake of being in bondage. Torment itself does not make us holy; trials in and of themselves do not make us holy. Rather, God meets us in our trials. Through faith we can grow closer to God by experiencing His goodness in spite of our pain, and in some cases, experience God's goodness and love through healing via various means. *As OCD sufferers, we must remind ourselves to cling to God and not our trial for sanctification.*

Galatians 5:1 says, *"It was for freedom that Christ set us free; therefore keep standing firm and do not be subject again to a yoke of slavery"* (NASB 1995). The yoke of slavery in this passage refers to the Mosaic law that Jews who believed Christ was the Messiah were tempted to follow. This is also referred to as legalism, which takes on different forms in Christianity today. The idea behind legalism is that we must earn God's favor through perfect behavior. Slavery and bondage to the law denies the freedom Christ died to give us. Rather than taking up our spiritual inheritance through faith, legalism asks us to remain slaves to worldly rules and expectations that we will never be able to fully satisfy.

Similarly, OCD sufferers may be tempted to remain as slaves to the disorder rather than seeking out opportunities for healing and freedom. It is a common human frailty to believe that self-inflicted torment produces righteousness and that righteousness can somehow be earned through pain, but Scripture teaches that righteousness is only found through faith in Christ Jesus who set us free from such bondage!

Escaping a trial in an un-biblical way can only happen if we escape through sin. For example, if a person is tempted to drink themselves into drunkenness, the temptation itself is the trial, and they must rely on God, other believers, and possibly even support groups for strength and grace to remove or withstand the temptation. A person can only remove the trial in their own strength by satisfying the temptation or replacing it with other sinful activities. The difference for OCD sufferers is abundantly clear. The use of medication is not a sinful act used to satisfy a temptation or to temporarily distract oneself from a trial through the satisfaction of fleshly desires. In fact, the result of medication can include a healthier brain able to remember God's promises and consistently trust in Him.

Persevering in a trial with God when there is no way to change the situation is an act of obedience and love. To remain in senseless bondage to a crippling disease when medicine is available—and to continue in fruitless self-torment—is destructive, wastes precious time, and is not what God intends for His beloved children.

My Life Without OCD Medication

Suppose that an all-healing medicine could be given for any disease on the planet. You know it, and all you have to do is use your needle to inject the liquid into your bloodstream. Unfortunately, your needle is defective. Sometimes, the injection goes through smoothly, but 99% of the time, you end up with a malfunction that hinders the injection process. You are unaware of the defect, so you seek advice. You approach your friends and say, "I'm not feeling so well, and I can't seem to get better." Their response is, "If only you'd take the medicine, you'd be better in a matter of days!" So, you take their advice, and try the injection 50 more times throughout the next week, yet you never get better. This leads you to conclude that you're the one "doing something wrong," and you feel so guilty and overwhelmed you don't know what to do.

This is how I lived in 2002, when I felt so condemned by my own thoughts that I was convinced even praying was a sin. Those around me said, "You need to just spend time with God. He is all-knowing and all-powerful, and He loves you and will change how you feel if you just trust Him." I would take the advice and try to spend time meditating on God's Word, only to feel more confused and condemned.

I felt as if I was looking through a doorway where I could see the immeasurable peace and joy of an infinitely loving God. I walked toward the doorway, only to be met by an invisible wall made of glass shards; I was left with a scratched-up face and was badly jarred by the experience. However, I could still see what the other side had to offer, so I brushed myself off and tried to walk through the doorway—over and over again. The harder I approached the doorway, the more the shards cut me. It wasn't a lack of faith or Bible knowledge causing the separation; it was a chemical imbalance that got me so wrapped up in "what-if" scenarios that I began to lose sight of reality.

People need a certain level of mental health to correctly perceive how they are to walk in step with the Spirit of God. I had a willing spirit but a broken brain. With the admonition to "just trust God more; He is faithful," I would think along these lines:

> *"Well, what that person is saying definitely makes sense according to my understanding of Scripture. However, because I'm in such terrible sin, my understanding of God's Word is so skewed that there is a chance I am misunderstanding His Word. To make things right, I need to repent. However, I am stuck because I do not know if my understanding of what I need to do to repent is indeed correct. After all, my understanding has potentially been skewed by my sinful actions. Therefore, I cannot read the scripture to find wisdom, nor can I pray."*

I have not exaggerated these thoughts. In my diseased state of mind, I could not make a simple, God-honoring decision to pray or to read His Word. Although I fully believed in God's ability to do anything, I thought I couldn't possibly be in a position to receive anything from Him. The feeling of self-condemnation was so oppressive that praying seemed impossible. I was unable to believe the power of God was for me, not because of a lack of faith, but because of a confused mind. The Holy Spirit was in me, but my brain just wasn't able to respond rationally. If we believe that we are transformed by the renewing of our minds, then I suggest we should do what we can to put our brains in as healthy a state as possible.

Peter cautioned this way: "*Therefore be self-controlled and sober-minded for the sake of your prayers*" (1 Peter 4:7b, ESV). The Greek word for sober-minded is *sōphroneō*, which means "to be of sound mind."[15] In this admonition from Peter, self-control and a sound mind are needed to pray effectively. In my case, I was able to achieve a sound mind with the help of medication—and then to pray effectively, without hindrance.

Some Reassurance

I want to leave those of you considering the use of medicine with a word of encouragement. You can use medicine without being absolutely convinced it is the right thing to do. You can do this without feeling condemned. You can do this without fearing that you are lacking in faith or perseverance. You can do this while still relying on God's grace. I cannot say for certain that medicine is always the right answer for everyone, but I do know for certain that we serve and live for a loving, compassionate God. He is slow to anger, and you must trust that if you decide to use medicine, He will guide you and make all things work together for your good—even your use of medicine.

With God, this issue comes down to a matter of the heart. An action done by one person may be sinful while another can do it in a way that pleases God. A foolish person who recklessly injures someone in an act of rage is in the wrong. However, a person who injures a burglar while in the process of protecting their family is doing what God would want them to do. Both people have injured someone, yet the righteousness of their actions is fully based on their heart's intent.

And so it is with medicine. Those who take medicine so they can walk away from God and stop trusting in God daily are in the wrong. However, those who take medicine so they can more readily experience God's power in their lives through a healthy mind made more in line with how it was created are not in sin. In my case, I chose to take medicine because I knew my brain was not sound and that I needed help to heal; I was in no way seeking to replace God's power in my life. If this is also your heart's desire, then I am confident that God is pleased with the intentions of your heart.

CHAPTER 6

THE POWER OF GOD'S WORD IN RECOGNIZING COGNITIVE ERRORS

This chapter briefly discusses some common patterns of thinking—or cognitive errors—commonly exhibited by OCD sufferers. These include an exaggerated or false burden of responsibility and the resulting compulsion to exert control, thinking that control will address the responsibility. I'll refer to these cognitive errors throughout the remainder of the book. Later in this chapter, I'll present some Scripture verses that can be helpful in managing some of these thinking patterns. However, it is God and His grace, not the compulsive use of Scripture, that helps us overcome. Meditation on these verses may need to be used in conjunction with counseling, prayer, medication, and the additional cognitive-behavioral suggestions presented in Chapter 4.[iv]

---

iv. In Chapters 8 and 9, I discuss our relationship with God and how to use His Word to discern whether thoughts are from Him or not.

OCD Exemplified

To illustrate OCD cognitive errors in my own thinking, let's turn to another basketball game at which I took pictures in college for my school newspaper.

As previously mentioned, sports photography is a great hobby and a joy to me. I'm a huge sports fan and relished the privilege and thrill of shooting collegiate athletics. I loved seeing my pictures in print in the college newspaper. However, relishing in any enjoyment of this hobby was always challenged by my OCD. From the start of my sports photography pursuits in college, I found reasons why photography might be a sin for me. I feared that it might turn into an idol and that it might make me fall away from my walk with God. Thus, after some brief experiences my freshman year, I decided to abstain from doing any sports photography for the first three years of college. Finally, in my senior year, I fought off my OCD thoughts long enough to dive back in.

One event I covered involved a glorious stadium introduction of the basketball team, a slam dunk contest, and a scrimmage. Despite my old fears that this activity would become an idol for me, I decided to take pictures and to bear the guilt that would come. Fortunately (and unfortunately), one of my shots from that night ended up on the front page of the school paper the next week. I distinctly remember it was a shot of a player wearing orange. My thoughts started to lean toward fear, and before I knew it, I was horrified. My thought process went something like this:

- What if it wasn't God's will that I take pictures at the game after all?
- If so, what if that picture being in the paper wasn't His will either?
- If so, what if He didn't protect all those involved in printing the picture from harm because, after all, it wasn't His will?

- If so, what if the ink ran out during the printing process and someone had to replace the orange cartridge? After all, there was a lot of orange color in that photo.
- If so, what if something terrible happened to that worker while he or she went to retrieve a new ink cartridge? Even worse, what if they were killed in an accident on their way to buy the cartridge?
- If so, I might be responsible for their death and all the other negative consequences resulting from my sinful choice!

Common Cognitive Errors by Dr. Mark Crawford

This example illustrates the common errors in OCD thinking as discussed in more detail by psychologist Mark Crawford, PhD, in his book, *The Obsessive-Compulsive Trap*. According to Crawford, OCD is often marked by these common cognitive errors: emotional reasoning, catastrophizing, dichotomous thinking, and personalization. His explanations of these cognitive errors are a great resource for OCD sufferers seeking to evaluate their own thoughts. In the following paragraphs, I will provide examples of these cognitive errors in my own thinking related to the example above.

According to Crawford, **emotional reasoning** occurs when feelings define the person's sense of reality rather than actual truth.[1] In the example above, my anxiety about whether I was outside God's will or was choosing an action that was displeasing to Him caused me to fear that I or someone else would be punished for my choice because God was angry with me. I completely dismissed the reality that my motives were pure and that I serve a loving, gracious God. I solely focused on the fear that what I did was wrong and displeasing to God. In this way, my emotions, not truth, defined my reality.

Catastrophizing is "imagining the worst-case scenario of a situation and reacting to the imagined 'catastrophe' rather than the actual situation. Their anxiety level matches the imagined catastrophe rather than the fact that nothing has happened."[2] In the example above, I imagined that an innocent person had been hurt or killed retrieving an ink cartridge because I was not in God's will to shoot photos at a basketball game.

In a common example, people without OCD may wonder at some point whether they locked their door, but they do not assume that not locking the door will lead to a catastrophe 99.9% of the time, so they can easily dismiss the concern. In contrast, someone with OCD considers the ramifications of the ten worst-case scenarios that will result from their failure to lock the door, and focuses on the potential catastrophes, reacting as if they are inevitabilities.

Dichotomous thinking is thinking in absolute terms (either-or thinking). Crawford says, "A person with OCD may have unrealistic standards for performance. Anything short of perfection is viewed as a failure."[3] Anyone with a hand-washing obsession needs no further explanation! This compulsion has no mercy, and the standard is perfection. Hands are either clean or contaminated. If they've just been washed but accidentally brush up against a wall, then they are contaminated. The compulsion to rewash our hands is as strong as if they had been smeared over a table just after someone sneezed on it. Why? Because hands are either perfectly clean or contaminated. There is no in-between. There is no "good enough."

Dichotomous thinking is a strong temptation for Christians with OCD because it is very similar to legalism, which contrives false standards to ensure righteousness and misses the *intent* of the law.

Personalization is the "tendency to make everything that happens somehow related to the person (i.e., "everything's my fault")."[4] This cognitive error is painfully apparent in my basketball photo example above. I was ready to ascribe the potential death of the person buying toner to my "mistake" of taking photos at the basketball game. Personalization creates self-blame, condemnation, and an overwhelming feeling of responsibility for an imagined negative outcome.

Selective attention is simply the tendency to focus on one aspect of a situation (usually a negative), no matter how minor it may be.[5] For example, in high school I noticed that students in class often mentioned they were so annoyed when a teacher erased the board but missed a little spot. In that situation, over 99% of the board had been properly erased, but some students could only focus on the less than 1% of the board that had not been erased.

In my basketball story, I focused only on the potential that I was wrong. I could not wrestle my attention to focus on the positives of the experience and what it might mean if I were not in the wrong. Selective attention has challenged me greatly over the course of my Christian life, as well, particularly when I study God's Word. Rather than finding comfort in the story of our Savior or in the stories of the great goodness and bountiful grace of our God, reading the Bible often becomes a battle over selective attention. Sometimes, I have struggled to avoid focusing solely on the verses that caused me confusion, feelings of condemnation, or led me to doubt God' goodness toward me. My grandfather, whom I often called with these concerns, lovingly told me one day that I was always looking for thorns. He described the Bible as a rose and described me as someone looking only for thorns instead of appreciating the beauty of the rose. What a great analogy for selective attention!

Responsibility and Control

Two distinctive features of OCD center on the issues of responsibility and control. Behind the question, "Did I lock the door this morning?" is the real fear, "Am I potentially responsible if something bad happens?" This is the crux of nearly every OCD cognitive error. We fear causing a fire, being the reason that our house will be robbed, living outside God's will, and so on. Here's a hypothetical example:

- We just used the bathroom.
- Our responsibility is to wash our hands.
- We immediately fear we will be responsible for contamination if we do not leave the bathroom adequately clean.
- The responsibility leaves us overwhelmed, so we try to control it as best we can, by scrubbing and scrubbing and rescrubbing just to make sure we don't mess up and contaminate someone or something.

No matter what scenario we face, more often than not, we convince ourselves that we have to take responsibility—which ultimately leads to a fear we will somehow fail at our responsibility, which then leads us to control. We use our compulsions to control the fear we have.

I like to think of people who have healthy emotional responses as having a correct emotional digestive tract. For example, in goes an injustice, and out comes anger. In goes a rude comment, out comes a statement asking for respect. In goes a tragic event, out comes grieving. In comes abusive treatment, out comes well-formed boundaries. (Of course, Christians can express these challenging emotions to God and respond in love. I am not justifying acting in unloving ways when these emotions arise. I only highlight that a balanced emotional response is honest and is careful both to respect others and to ask for respect from others.)

However, as OCD sufferers, we might find that our emotional digestive tract produces control far more than anything else. I am wronged, out comes control. I get hurt, out comes control. I am treated unfairly, out comes control. I am shown disrespect, out comes control. I am treated abusively, out comes control. If I feel fear, out comes control. And back to our example, if I feel responsible for any number of calamities—contamination or injury or even death, out comes my attempt to control in the form of compulsions.

To simplify, all OCD sufferers have a common pattern of cognitive errors that consistently arise in their thoughts and behaviors:

- Compulsions are rooted in overwhelming feelings of ultimate responsibility.
- Anxiety from the gravity of ultimate responsibility drives an obsessive need to control.
- The underlying sense that I can do something to control an outcome (e.g., prevent disaster) reflects an inflated sense of responsibility.
- Obsession with ultimate responsibility and control replaces trust in God's sovereignty.

Scriptural Counterpunches to Common Cognitive Errors

My use of God's Word has often been like one who takes a shovel and tries to dig a hole using the handle instead of the shovel head. More times than I can count, I have found myself immersed in God's Word, searching for and finding condemnation, rather than believing God's promises and receiving His blessings and hope. I've often feared that I am a lost soul incapable of receiving salvation, or a saved soul so entrapped in sin that walking peacefully with God becomes impossible. But I hope my fellow OCD sufferers can find hope in and learn from my experience. Despite all these very significant challenges to my meditations on Scripture, God has still guided me, taught me, and ministered to me by His Word. My hope is that the following Scriptures bless other OCD sufferers as they have me, enabling each of us to battle the common cognitive errors that are the foundation for all OCD obsessions and compulsions.

Emotional Reasoning: Take the Thought Captive

The weapons we fight with are not the weapons of the world. On the contrary, they have divine power to demolish strongholds. We demolish arguments and every pretension that sets itself up against the knowledge of God, and we take captive every thought to make it obedient to Christ (2 Corinthians 10:4–5).

People with OCD must realize that their *feeling* is a speculation (pretension) and that they are letting their obsession assume an exalted position in their minds and lives. According to this verse, both the speculation that our hands are dirty after shaking someone's hand and the complete submission to this obsession must be destroyed. How?

We are children of God, created in His image, and we have the ability to choose (by the use of our will) to follow our emotions or to follow God's Word. *Our will has power over our emotions, not the other way around.* I do not say this to be trite, or to ignore the fuel that OCD provides to make this difficult. In the same way that we can choose to not kill or steal no matter how mad or tempted we become, so we can choose to not give in to a compulsion no matter how obsessed we are with doing so. We must make the decision to give neither the thought of dirtiness nor the obsession any place in our lives. I know this is easier said that done, and my intent is not to gloss over the hurdles we face in doing this. Chapter 8 details additional strategies to combine with taking our thoughts, feelings, and fears captive. The key is to recognize that the feeling is caused by OCD (and not our own desires) and to refocus our attention on an enjoyable activity.

In my example of taking photographs, the fear of sinning against God could have been stemmed if I had shared my feelings with a trustworthy believer. An external viewpoint would have helped me recognize and separate my emotions from the reality of the situation. Second, I could have practiced refocusing my emotions onto the ultimate reality, that God's grace and favor are toward me.

Catastrophizing and Personalization: Rejoice in the Lord and Pray with Thanksgiving

> *Rejoice in the Lord always. Again I will say, rejoice! Let your gentleness be known to all men. The Lord is at hand. Be anxious for nothing, but in everything by prayer and supplication, with thanksgiving, let your requests be made known to God; and the peace of God, which surpasses all understanding, will guard your hearts and minds through Christ Jesus.*
>
> —Philippians 4:4–7

There will always be remote possibilities of a catastrophe happening. However, I feel that the only way to overcome this is to realize that even in the case of a catastrophe, God is eternally good and will take care of us. God does not tell us to not worry because bad things will never happen; we are not to worry because He cares for us even when bad things do happen. *"And we know that all things work together for good to those who love God, to those who are the called according to His purpose"* (Romans 8:28). As we get in the habit of meditating on Scriptures that remind us of God's goodness, faithfulness, and favor toward us, transformation will occur (Romans 12:2). Consider these Scriptures:

- *"My flesh and my heart fail; but God is the* ***strength*** *of my heart and my portion forever"* (Psalm 73:26, emphasis added).
- *"For I am persuaded that neither death nor life, nor angels nor principalities nor powers, nor things present nor things to come, nor height nor depth, nor any other created thing, shall be able to separate us from the love of God which is in Christ Jesus our Lord"* (Romans 8:38–39).

With a renewed mind, my prayer and thought process regarding sports photography should have gone something like this:

> *"Thank you, Lord, for allowing me to find so much joy in photography. Thank you for providing the opportunity to work for the school paper and for giving me access to all the equipment needed to do a good job. Although I am nervous that having my photography published may lead to people being injured or killed, I know that You are good and are in control. You have my very best at heart, and Your purposes are always good. You love me more than I could ever love You or anyone else. You know that I am afraid for others' safety, and I give that fear to You, not carrying it myself. Your Word says that I should cast all my anxieties on You because You care for me (1 Peter 5:7). Jesus said, "Do not let your hearts be troubled and do not be afraid" (John 14:27c). Therefore, Lord, I entrust You with the lives of those who are working on printing the newspaper tonight. In the unlikely event that some of them are injured or worse, I know that You can use that for good, and that*

> *Your ways are higher than my own. Help me not to focus on that possibility but to focus on You, trusting in You. Thank You for making me Your child, and for constantly showering me with Your grace even when I don't obey or make the right decisions. Help me to go through my day always remembering that You hold me in Your hands and treat me with more love than I could ever express. Finally, God, if anything I do displeases You, I know You will reveal that to me in gentleness and kindness through more than my own mind. You will be faithful to show me and teach me, even if I don't understand at first. I know Your Truth will come from places other than the fruit of my own fears."*

For those feeling too guilty or condemned to even pray, remember that we can pray because of God's grace and not our own faithfulness and obedience. One of my favorite verses comes from the book of Hebrews:

> *For we do not have a High Priest who cannot sympathize with our weaknesses, but was in all points tempted as we are, yet without sin. Let us therefore come boldly to the* throne of grace, *that we may obtain mercy and find grace to help in time of need.*
>
> —Hebrews 4:15–16 (emphasis added)

And finally, for those in such an intense state of confusion to even pray, the Spirit of God is with you and interceding for you:

> *Likewise the Spirit also helps in our weaknesses. For we do not know what we should pray for as we ought, but the Spirit Himself makes intercession for*

> *us with groanings which cannot be uttered. Now He who searches the hearts knows what the mind of the Spirit is, because He makes intercession for the saints according to the will of God.*
>
> —Romans 8:26–27

> *But He, because He continues forever, has an unchangeable priesthood. Therefore He is also able to save to the uttermost those who come to God through Him, since He always lives to make intercession for them.*
>
> —Hebrews 7:24–25[v]

Dichotomous Thinking: Consider What Is Reasonable and Affirm the Character of God

> *But the wisdom from above is first pure, then peaceable, gentle, reasonable,* full of *mercy and good fruit, unwavering, without hypocrisy.*
>
> —James 3:17 (NASB 1995)[vi]

Thoughts such as "the 99% I got on my test is not good enough," and "my hands might be moderately clean, but they are not completely clean, so I *have* to wash them again," do not reflect any of the words defining wisdom as listed in James 3:17. The word I love the most in that verse is *reasonable*. Dichotomous thinking is simply not reasonable. Dichotomous thinking is

---

v. If you don't know what truth to pray for or how to find it in God's Word, ask some trusted Christian friends, Christian counselors, or pastors. Try a word search on Bible search engines such as biblegateway.com. Also see Chapter 8 in this book.

vi. See section entitled "The Bible Promises That the Word Can Provide Discernment" in Chapter 8 for a more detailed application of this verse.

based on the belief that lasting perfection can be reached. We all know there is no perfect state of perfection on this earth. An OCD sufferer may wash their hands so perfectly that they can relax knowing they are completely clean—for a moment. But this transitory state is in and of itself unreasonable because it is impossible to maintain. Our God does not ask us to be a slave to such unreasonable demands.

Another major lie of dichotomous thinking is that the thing we are trying to perfect won't change. Let's say we get our hands 100% clean. Tomorrow, the compulsion may change from needing 100% clean hands to needing to say hello perfectly to every person we see, or to responding perfectly to people in every situation we face. These torturous patterns are anything but reasonable and free of hypocrisy. They indirectly imply that we can get to a state in which we are able to do something perfectly all the time, which is essentially believing that we have transcended the confines of this earth!

The very fact that Christ came to earth to die for our sins is a testimony that God knows we humans *cannot* be perfect. He does not ask that of us. We must realize that God knows our frailties and gently shepherds and loves us despite all our shortcomings.

> *As far as the east is from the west, so far has He removed our transgressions from us. As a father pities his children, so the LORD pities those who fear Him. For He knows our frame; He remembers that we are dust. As for man, his days are like grass; as a flower of the field, so he flourishes. For the wind passes over it, and it is gone, and its place remembers it no more. But the mercy of the LORD is from everlasting to everlasting on those who fear Him, and His righteousness to children's children.*
>
> —Psalm 103:12–17

The description of love in 1 Corinthians 13 also shows us how much God acknowledges our lack of perfection—as love bears all things and endures all things. None of us can live up to the standard of holiness that God has. People who struggle with dichotomous thinking must immerse themselves in the verses that demonstrate the frailty of mankind and testify that the mercies and sovereignty of God are the things to rely on, not our human performance.

Because we are Christians and because we contend with OCD, it can cause us to misinterpret what God wants from us in His Word. We may try to fulfill God's commands but end up trapped in habitual thought patterns that lead us to believe we must do things precisely, in an exact order, at an exact time, or for an exact amount of time. All the while, we are likely saddening God, because we are looking at the letter of His law and not the intent or spirit of His law. His laws are not meant to be burdensome, and He is not harsh with us:

> *Not that we are sufficient of ourselves to think of anything as being from ourselves, but our sufficiency is from God, who also made us sufficient as ministers of the new covenant,* ***not of the letter but of the Spirit; for the letter kills, but the Spirit gives life.***
>
> —2 Corinthians 3:5–6 (emphasis added)[vii]

In our attempt to please God, selective attention makes us forget His greatest commands:

> *Jesus answered him, "The first of all the commandments is: 'Hear, O Israel, the Lord our God, the Lord is one. And you shall love the Lord your God with all*

---

vii. I expound more on this verse in Chapter 8, section entitled "The Bible Promises That the Word Can Provide Discernment".

> *your heart, with all your soul, with all your mind, and with all your strength.' This is the first commandment. And the second, like it, is this: 'You shall love your neighbor as yourself.' There is no other commandment greater than these."*
>
> —Mark 12:29–32

Selective Attention: Set Your Mind on Things Above

> *Finally, brothers and sisters, whatever is true, whatever is noble, whatever is right, whatever is pure, whatever is lovely, whatever is admirable—if anything is excellent or praiseworthy—think about such things.*
>
> —Philippians 4:8 (NIV)

> *If then you were raised with Christ, seek those things which are above, where Christ is, sitting at the right hand of God. Set your mind on things above, not on things on the earth. For you died, and your life is hidden with Christ in God.*
>
> —Colossians 3:1–3

Selectively paying attention to things that are untrue or speculative can lead to an exacerbation of OCD. Whether it be fear of evil or condemnation or a fear of being out of God's will, paying attention solely to these fears and lies will lead to more selective attention. If you tend to have this type of thinking, it is vital that you notice it while it is happening and recognize the train of thought as not only destructive but stemming from untrue or speculative thinking. Additionally, focusing on something good, true, and praiseworthy instead of the fear and anxiety will help train our minds as God intended.

Responsibility and Control: Rest in Christ

"Come to Me, all you *who labor and are heavy laden, and I will give you rest"* (Matthew 11:28). God truly does want us to trust Him, no matter how condemned, far from Him, or out of His will we may feel. The key to doing this is learning to transfer all the responsibility we feel from ourselves to God. We must make the transfer no matter how much OCD condemns us and demands that we strive for perfection and for righteousness, or demands that we enslave ourselves to rituals to prevent catastrophe, or demands that we take control. Believing and trusting in God's faithfulness, goodness, and grace is key to freeing one from OCD's grasp.

CHAPTER 7

OCD IN RELATIONSHIPS – THE NEED FOR CONTROL AND COMMUNITY

"A new commandment I give to you, that you love one another; as I have loved you, that you also love one another."

—John 13:34

Be kindly affectionate to one another with brotherly love, in honor giving preference to one another.

—Romans 12:10

This chapter focuses on how OCD plays out in our relationships and why we so desperately need to be connected to others in the body of Christ as a means of battling and overcoming this disorder. When considering how OCD manifests in relationships, I think that the biggest challenge is control. As OCD sufferers, we feel enslaved to rituals of control—obsessions that try to rule our thoughts and compulsions and that war to rule our behaviors.

The bystanders to this struggle—those whom we love and need the most—often become ensnared in the control of this disease. Sometimes, these bystanders are the subject of our obsessive-compulsive behaviors, or get in the way of such behaviors or inadvertently trigger such behaviors. The end result of any of these scenarios is the same: we may attempt to control those around us in small or big ways or resort to avoidance in order to stop this cycle. This can be confusing, upsetting, exasperating, and alienating to those around us. At the same time that we push others away through our need to control them, we desperately crave encouragement and wisdom from our loved ones, friends, and most especially, the body of Christ. Understanding OCD's relationship with control—how it manifests, why it manifests, how to recognize the behavior as OCD, and how best to combat it through biblical teachings—is the key to preserving healthy relationships.

Why OCD Sufferers Control

For the OCD sufferer, others can help them climb out of an OCD spiral, or they can inadvertently say or do something that sends them into a spiral. The situation is complicated and challenging for all involved, but despite the complexity and endless ways this cycle may manifest, the key to greater understanding is this: The OCD sufferer's greatest burden is their sense of responsibility and/or their driving need to prevent pain—whether it be emotional, spiritual, or temporal. The cycle can encompass the great breadth of painful and frightening human experiences of every intensity—from insult to confusion to shame to abuse to contamination to illness to disasters to catastrophes to eternal damnation and more. This overwhelming and debilitating need manifests itself in controlling behaviors, avoidance, and isolation.

How OCD Sufferers Control in Relationships

When I consider the way I allowed my OCD tendency toward control to affect my relationships, I shudder. At times, I would not allow family members to eat, swallow, or chew in my presence; further, I objected to the mention of specific words or thoughts, demanded that others clean themselves or not touch certain objects, and so on. In the body of Christ, I have experienced the temptation to avoid certain people, ideas, or situations. I have acted on compulsions while in the presence of others, which has confused them and likely induced them to question my intentions. All this, I would argue, was driven by my need to control pain and to limit any potential dangers to me emotionally or spiritually. One of the most entrenched OCD strategies I learned from childhood to render control and accomplish my mission of pain prevention was born in a close personal relationship—my tumultuous relationship with my father. I call this strategy a "misdirected OCD boundary."

My father could be kind, gentle, funny and generous. He even used his creativity and charisma to bring attention to wrongly persecuted people in other countries through some of his powerful acquaintances in the Washington, DC area. And although I know he loved me, he sometimes had a hard time controlling his temper. This negatively impacted me, especially as a child, and left me unable to process the strong emotions that resulted from his behaviors. I didn't know how to recognize that my father could actually be wrong in his treatment of me or how to stop blaming myself for the way he treated me when he was angry. My line of thinking went something like this:

> *"I am a sinner saved by grace. I am called to forgive others as I have been forgiven. My father just became very angry toward me and treated me poorly.*

> *Therefore, I must be deserving of this treatment. After all, if it weren't for the grace of God, I would never receive favor in anything."*

As you can see, this made forgiving my father very easy because in my mind, he really didn't do anything wrong. Even though my mind was convinced that I had been treated fairly, my heart surely was not. As I grew older, the anger in my heart began to build and manifest itself through a fixation on certain sounds and mannerisms. I noticed that the sound of my father swallowing began to get under my skin. It became increasingly difficult to be in a room with him, for fear that I would hear him swallow. And I recognized something: "*I might not be able to control how my father treats me when he gets upset about something, but I sure can control whether I hear that swallow of his.*" While I legitimately desired to set healthy boundaries with my father that would prevent him from treating me poorly when angry, that was beyond my power. So, I created a boundary that gave me a false sense of control over him—which I call a "misdirected OCD boundary." This way of thinking is similar to saying, "I may not be able to control all the germs on this planet, but I sure can control the ones on my hands." I knew I could not control my father's angry behaviors, but I pinpointed one thing that I knew I could control—allowing myself to endure the sound of his swallow. I did my absolute best to make sure that I controlled situations so that I did not suffer that one behavior whenever possible. This misdirected boundary did little to address my actual source of suffering; it's possible it actually increased my father's anger toward me, but it gave me an imagined sense of control and, therefore, false comfort.

I started by not allowing my father to swallow behind me, as I couldn't stand the thought of letting him make a sound outside my line of sight. It quickly became acceptable in my mind to not allow myself to hear him swallow at all, leading me to cover my ears at the dinner table whenever I felt like it. Eventually, the moment he entered a room, I would cover my ears with my hands, a pillow, or the sleeve of my shirt. Being in the same room with him became so unbearable to me that it was nearly impossible to function normally in a relationship with him. The next time his anger would flare, I would cling to that wrong as a way to justify my behavior all the more.

This is just one example of how I have struggled with controlling all manner of behaviors of those closest to me at times. One thing I have learned through all this is that control is a double-edged sword. As much as we crave control to alleviate our burden of responsibility, control hurts us by alienating those we need the most. We need healthy relationships with family and friends and the body of Christ as we battle OCD. When controlling behaviors increase, we engage community less.

Understanding the OCD Cycle of Control in Relationships

The following 2 steps are experienced by most people who have been treated unjustly:

1. **A triggering circumstance occurs.** These are real, valid triggering events, such as being hurt in an argument or being treated unfairly at work. Example: Being treated harshly by my father was such a triggering circumstance.
2. **Emotions form as a result of the circumstance.** Valid emotional responses result from the triggering circumstance. Example: When my father was unreasonably harsh or impatient with me, I would get angry.

The following steps are what occur when the OCD process kicks in. I credit my wife with this excellent explanation of how the process works in me. I will reference the example of how I responded to my father to help illustrate each step.

3. **Emotions intensify and multiply.** I've learned that the emotions I experience in response to a wrong done to me are usually multiplied several times in intensity compared to the reaction of someone without OCD. Example: When my father lashed out at me, I not only felt hurt, but I would also obsess over the situation, which only multiplied my pain. This left me hurt at a level that was often unbearable, all-consuming, and difficult to overcome.
4. **Worry, introspection, and self-doubt set in.** A person with OCD will involuntarily be stuck in these ways of thinking following a triggering event—and to an intense degree. Example: Thinking to myself, "*What did I do to hurt my father like this? Why didn't I do things exactly as he asked? Should I try to make things right?*"
5. **The impulse to control kicks in.** Strong emotional responses of hurt, pain, worry, and self-doubt often trigger OCD and the compulsion to control some aspect of the triggering circumstances.

   Example: "*I am upset by my father's treatment of me. I cannot control my father. I do not know how to handle my pain, worry, and fear. I cannot tell my father that I do not like how he treated me.*" I want to set legitimate boundaries on his bad behaviors, but I lack the ability to control my universe. Without better options, I established a misdirected boundary of control. I do not like the sound of my father's swallowing. I can't control him, but I can control his ability to make me suffer by swallowing.

6. **The compulsion to control grows as it is reinforced through repeated behaviors that lend a false sense of power to prevent pain.** We cling to our controlling compulsions toward others in order to somehow manufacture circumstances to control their ability to hurt or stress us. The energy from our pain, worry, and fear is redirected into our compulsions, and we let our compulsions continue to rule our mind, only to see them strengthened further on repeat. The more we use our compulsions to manage (or disguise) our pain and fear, the more we justify our compulsions as acceptable behaviors. This process, on repeat, validates the compulsion and increases our dependence on the compulsion as a means to prevent or assuage our discomfort.

   Example: I felt justified in avoiding my father's presence because he might swallow around me. In this way, I retained some shred of control over when and how he hurt me, falsely convincing myself on some level that the compulsion was a useful and powerful tool to protect myself.

To end this cycle of control, we must train ourselves to recognize its signs. What are the compulsions we have toward others that scream of control? When we realize these compulsions, we must acknowledge them and use the "Relabel" method that Dr. Schwartz discovered and outlined in *Brain Lock*.[1] He states that we have the ability to recognize when we are having an issue because of OCD, and not an external force or person.[viii]

In my example, I could have acknowledged that "The problem is not my father's swallowing; it's my OCD. I am attempting to control something to prevent pain. What is the real, legitimate pain I am attempting to prevent through control? How is OCD coming into

viii. See more on this topic in Chapter 8.

play? What behavior am I attempting to control, and does it address the real, legitimate pain I have suffered? Is this a misdirected OCD boundary? That is, will preventing my father from swallowing around me really prevent me from experiencing the hurt from his anger? There is power in recognizing the real problem that has triggered the OCD cycle and the reasons we have let OCD enter into our relationship. The more we understand the false promises of our rituals and compulsions, the greater power we have over them.

Attempting to Control for Pain in Relationships

Everyone has a desire to avoid pain in relationships. It is a natural impulse to protect oneself and those we love. For OCD sufferers, however, the burden of responsibility is extreme, and our belief in our ability to control pain can be highly over-exaggerated in our minds due to the disorder. One key to overcoming our debilitating fears is to recognize and dwell on spiritual truths that transfer our sense of responsibility to prevent pain in relationships from ourselves and back to God.

The obsessive fear of pain is so central to the thought patterns of OCD sufferers that it can be hard for them to transfer their responsibility to prevent bad things from happening to a God who, at times, may allow suffering as a part of His perfect plan. But God's character traits of omniscience, kindness, and goodness—coupled with His unending favor toward us—can be the greatest reassurance that He will be with us in the midst of pain in relationships. Our attempts to control our obsessions through compulsions alienate those with whom we desperately want to be in close, harmonious relationships. By dwelling on the goodness, kindness, grace, and limitless power of our loving Father, we can rightly rest in the reassurance that He will work all things together for His glory and our blessing—*independent of our ability to perfectly navigate human relationships.*

The following Scriptures are powerful truths to meditate on when, due to pain or the fear of pain, we need to be reminded of our God's goodness and faithfulness:

- *"When my father and my mother forsake me, Then the LORD will take care of me"* (Psalm 27:10).
- *"And we know that all things work together for good to those who love God, to those who are the called according to His purpose"* (Romans 8:28).
- *"But as for you, you meant evil against me; but God meant it for good, in order to bring it about as it is this day, to save many people alive"* (Genesis 50:20).
- *"For I know the thoughts that I think toward you, says the Lord, thoughts of peace and not of evil, to give you a future and a hope"* (Jeremiah 29:11).
- *"My flesh and my heart may fail, but God is the strength of my heart and my portion forever"* (Psalm 73:26).
- *"The Lord is near to those who have broken heart, and saves such as have a contrite spirit"* (Psalm 34:18).
- *"He heals the brokenhearted and binds up their wounds"* (Psalm 147:3).

Walking in the fullness of healthy relationships is made easier when we are no longer crippled by fear of pain. Since no human relationship can exist in a state of perfection, our place of rest and reassurance can be found in the perfect love of our Heavenly Father who will never fail us even when we, or those around us, fail.

Recognizing the Power We Have to Forgive in Relationships

Once we recognize that misdirected boundaries can't protect us from pain and that it is not our responsibility to prevent pain in relationships (nor can we do so), we can begin to understand what is under our control. Christ's example is the most powerful truth and foundational promise underpinning our faith, and as His followers, we are commanded to forgive. Ephesians 4:31–32 states:

> *Let all bitterness, wrath, anger, clamor, and evil speaking be put away from you, with all malice. And be kind to one another, tenderhearted, forgiving one another, even as God in Christ forgave you.*

However, forgiveness can be uniquely challenging for OCD sufferers. In fact, one of the most vicious cycles of condemnation in my life was related to forgiveness. Since OCD is so good at condemning its victims, it is very easy for victims to turn around and condemn others. We are so well trained on condemnation that I sometimes call us "professional self-condemners." As a Christian, I know unforgiveness is not godly, so I further condemn myself for not showing others grace, understanding, and forgiveness. In a moment and in one mind, I can swiftly condemn others and then be overcome with self-condemnation over this fact.

I have been severely beaten down by this passage: *"For if you forgive men their trespasses, your heavenly Father will also forgive you. But if you do not forgive men their trespasses, neither will your Father forgive your trespasses"* (Matthew 6:14–15). I knew that I was still God's child, as He calls us His children in the same verse in which He gives this warning, but I was concerned that my relationship with God couldn't be what it should be if I did not forgive. I felt helpless; if I couldn't forgive in my own strength, how could I expect God to forgive me with respect to my daily communion with Him? *It was as if God's power was victorious over every sin* except *unforgiveness.* Sins against me would play in my head over and over again and make me feel like a constant victim, while I simultaneously drowned in self-condemnation over my unforgiveness. I would then feel far from God because of this passage, and I was convinced that I was living in sin for not forgiving.

The lie I believed was rooted in my understanding of forgiveness. God finally showed me that my intense emotions and thoughts in response to a wrong are not what I am responsible for. All God asks of me is to decide in my heart to forgive—to no longer seek revenge, to keep no record of wrongs. When the intense feelings and thoughts of hurt rush into my mind, I can give those to God and ask Him to help me have victory over them. It may *feel* as if I am not forgiving, but I can acknowledge that *I have chosen to forgive.* I am not left on my own—without close fellowship with Him—in those moments. Rather, it is during those moments of temptation to get even that I should acknowledge my flesh is weak and craves vengeance, but my will is to forgive no matter the emotions I am feeling. The key is to ask God for victory over the painful memories and emotions. As Hannah Whitall Smith observed, we don't have to fall for the lie:

> Oh, how wicked you must be to think of such things! It is very plain that you are not trusting the Lord; for if you had been, it would have been impossible for these things to have entered your heart.[2]

Dr. Tony Evans, who holds a doctorate of theology and has written an entire Bible Commentary, defines forgiveness this way: "Forgiveness is not pretending like it didn't happen or it didn't hurt. That's lying. Forgiveness is the decision to release a debt regardless of how you feel."[3] Forgiveness is done by the will; the emotions will fall in line eventually, but the "when" is not our burden to carry, but the Lord's. And once this realization sets in, we can refocus on the unconditional grace God continues to give us. This eventually leads to a natural love for others, which leads to one of the most powerful and unique demonstrations of love we can display to a fallen world—namely, showing grace and forgiveness to others.

Control Is Not Loving or Kind to Ourselves and Rarely Understood by Others

Understanding the urge to control and what motivates it is the key for both OCD sufferers and those who support them. The OCD sufferer's feelings of intense responsibility to prevent an imagined worst-case scenario motivates their impulse to control. This extends not just to impositions we create for ourselves to perform, but also impositions we place on others. As I detailed in Chapter 2, I used to struggle with incessant cleaning rituals. As a result of my obsession with cleanliness, I never wanted people in my room. If they touched certain items or even the floor with their hands, I would be almost panic-stricken. Why? Because I had lost complete control of how the "contamination" might affect the rest of the home or even the outside community. I would often end up yelling at my siblings or even parents until they washed their hands.

The following is not at all meant to condemn, but rather to show a way to freedom. OCD is sometimes intertwined with our sinful flesh. It may come in the form of control or a belief that we can make things right via a ritual. Whatever the reason, it is most important to realize what we are *not* doing when we give in to obeying an obsession and performing a compulsion. We are *not* believing what God says is true because we are *not* hoping in God's care for us; we are *not* loving ourselves (or others, as demonstrated above); and we are *not* living as God asked us to live in Micah 6:8: *"He has shown you, O man, what is good; and what does the Lord require of you but to do justly, to love mercy, and to walk humbly with your God?"*

Think of how out of place this verse seems with respect to the example of how I controlled access to my room! If you give in to OCD and simultaneously try to apply this verse, you will find it impossible. Doing justice must involve others—namely fighting for the justice of others or treating others in a just way. And the same goes for loving mercy. How can you be merciful to others or even to yourself when you are focusing on obsessive thoughts or urges? You can't! When we decide to obey God's call in Micah 6:8, we immediately destroy any place for these compulsions because those compulsive urges make us focus on demanding of ourselves, instead of acting fairly and generously toward others.

Once we recognize (as Paul did) that we have a flesh that wars against the Spirit of God who lives in us, we can begin attributing our OCD thoughts to the flesh. We can have peace knowing that when we reject OCD compulsions, we are actually stepping out in faith and believing that God's Word is true. Having this knowledge is vital to our fight against OCD.

How to Help Others Help Us

When I first began to fear I could lose my salvation, I went through the entire New Testament and made a list of every verse or passage I thought could potentially confirm my thinking. When I went to my grandfather for explanations of these verses, he often went on explaining the historical context of the Scriptures—who was really being addressed, and so on. This preponderance of information often left me feeling frustrated. All I really wanted and needed was a direct response as to whether the verses gave me a responsibility to make sure I didn't *do* something that could make me lose my salvation.

Most people do not realize what we are going through and what we need to help us get past our compulsive issues.

To help others understand and help us, we must explain our primary need; that is, our need is to be assured that we are not responsible for preventing pain. When we are trapped in a cycle of obsessions and compulsions, we forget that this cycle is related to our fear of pain and catastrophe and the sense that we are responsible for preventing these dangers from becoming a reality. And we sometimes forget to tell others that this is the reason why we do what we do. People may not understand OCD, but they understand fear. OCD is unique in that it makes our fears much more intense than what the average person experiences because it inflates (extremely intensely) our sense of responsibility. However, everyone experiences fear and can relate to that emotion.

Let's return to the example given in the Introduction about a child fearing for his parents' safety and associating his behavior with their departure for work, and hence the possibility that they would be in a car accident. The child may simply say to his parents, "I have to read my Bible, or bad things will happen." Most parents would say, "No, that's a silly thought, and you know that's not true." The parents would find the thought absurd and irrational and would likely have few tools to combat it other than outright dismissal. This response will likely leave the child frustrated and more agitated. The problem is that as OCD sufferers, we too often expect people to understand the reasoning behind our final conclusion, which in our minds, is based on logic and therefore has validity. (And in this example, it is a child with OCD who may not have the full verbal and cognitive skills to explain himself.)

Therefore, we need to provide more detail of what we fear. We need to ask for the other person's time and attention so we can describe our reasoning. In preparation, it is helpful to write out a step-by-step thought progression. Take the time to think through your fears, even if you have to work backward from the final conclusion. If the child is able to express himself, the reasons may flow as follows:

- Original fear: "My parents might get into a car accident on their way to work. They could end up hurt or dead!"
- "I should have been nicer to my parents this morning because maybe they would have decided to stay home with me and thus would avoid potentially being in a car accident."
- "The way I talk to my parents in the morning will determine whether they go to work and thus get into a car accident: I am responsible for preventing them from having a car accident."
- "If I had more joy in the Lord, I would have been nicer to my parents; therefore, I should read my Bible longer each morning."
- Compulsion: "I will read the Bible for 30 minutes each morning; therefore, my parents won't get into a car accident. I must do this perfectly, without bad thoughts or interruption."

Spelling out our thoughts in this way helps others give advice that takes the original fear into consideration—one they more than likely can relate to and have experienced themselves. Further, they can see the underlying lie behind the compulsion and address it head-on and tell us what we really need to hear—that we are not responsible! In this example, if the parents had seen this list of thoughts, they may have been better able to comfort their child and help him end his compulsion. The child really needed to experience (1) sympathy and understanding for his original fear, (2) reassurance that nothing he did had any impact on his parents' safety, and (3) direct affirmation that he was not responsible for their safety. Finally, he needed to have his thinking redirected to God's promises that He is good and gracious toward him—*independent of his ability to act perfectly or even acceptably.* The parents can help establish two essential facts:

- They were going to leave the house and head for work no matter how nicely or terribly behaved the child was that morning.
- In the event they did stay home for the child, nothing he did or didn't do would impact whether the parents would remain safe.

His fears won't be assuaged until he is convinced that there are no negative consequences from his behavior that could impact his parents' safety.

Beyond this, those close to us need to understand that as much as we know OCD is our tormentor, we somehow find solace in our disorder. "These walls are funny. First you hate 'em, then you get used to 'em. Enough time passes, you get so you depend on them. That's institutionalized."[4] This statement is made by a prisoner in a movie describing what prison does to people over time, which I find to be ironically similar to how OCD feels for sufferers. OCD sufferers hate having OCD and would do almost anything to rid themselves of it. But after a while, we subconsciously find safety in it, as it systematically engulfs our freedom and offers a false sense of control and protection from specific fears. Like the prisoner, we acknowledge that OCD is bondage, that it tortures us, and that we desire freedom from the crippling obsessions and compulsions. However, after years of suffering, it becomes what we know; and relinquishing control, no matter how freeing it may seem, can be scary. Others need to be aware that, deep down, OCD sufferers may fear victory because victory means relinquishing control, and control gives a sense of safety, no matter how misleading. Those trying to help us need to understand this attachment and remind OCD sufferers that a loving God is in control and that a false sense of responsibility is enslaving them.

This should be no surprise as it is the same problem we all have as sinners. When we come to know Christ, we know that His ways are infinitely better than ours. Yet even those who have spent their entire lives pursuing God struggle with clinging to the sinful flesh. It's what we know, no matter how inferior a choice it is compared with surrendering to the will of God. But God can give us the power, through His grace and great love for us, to let go of our devotion to thoughts and behaviors that enslave us.

Recognizing the Gift of the Body of Christ

Knowing someone actually understands and has experienced what you are going through is a relief and therapeutic in and of itself. It doesn't need to be a scholar or professional counselor, just someone who understands your thought processes. Someone who is able to speak truth and logic into your life and guide you through renewing your mind when your emotions are running high. This is where the body of Christ can play a powerful role in the life of OCD sufferers.

For a long time, I avoided sharing my struggles with OCD. That was mostly because when I did try, one of my greatest fears usually came true: most people couldn't relate to my issues. Even close friends and family members didn't really "get it," which left me with many negative emotions. Therefore, I tried to hide the issue. *"If people can't understand it, then I will learn to overcome it all on my own,"* I concluded. In addition, to make sure I would never be close enough to someone who could deeply hurt me, I kept everyone as far away as I possibly could. Again, control had reared its ugly head.

I even began to look down on others who shared their problems in community, seeing that as a weakness and a fault. I judged others for the foolishness of relying on fallible people instead of God. I have since seen the immaturity and mistake in my attitude. It's easy to choose isolation from others because of the guilt and shame we may feel because of OCD.

A counselor once told me that healthy people have an inner circle of people with whom they are most intimate—usually a counselor, God, and maybe their spouse. They then have a circle of very good friends, ones they will likely have for life. The circles grow outwardly to include acquaintances on the outermost circle. When the circles were being described to me, something hit me like a ton of bricks. There was only one person in my inner circle apart from my family and wife—my best friend Tim. I had pushed everyone else to the outermost rings of the circle. Sure, I had lots of friends, but only one really knew my daily pains, struggles, and challenges. The more I learn about myself, the more I realize that I have put up walls to protect myself from my deepest fears.

Despite the times I isolated, God blessed me with my late grandfather, my mother, and one of my best friends to vent to, lean on, and gain wisdom from. He has also sent me wise Christian counselors throughout my life. And as of 16 years ago, I was blessed with a wife who is more caring, loving, understanding, and wise than I will ever deserve. I have learned much from each of these people, and I have much more to learn. Shortly after getting married, it became clear to me that I was terrible at carrying the burdens of my wife—and other friends and family in my life—who so lovingly carried mine. Without the generosity and patience of these people, I don't know if I would be the person I am today.

No matter how much victory I experience over OCD in my life, there is no doubt that fellowship with the body of Christ is a critical part of the solution to fighting this disorder. We need to connect to the body of Christ in an authentic way, sharing our weaknesses. We need to allow others to encourage us and to be part of the body of Christ in our lives. We need to persevere in the hope of finding those who truly care and will listen. We may also learn how to better love others in their weaknesses and trials, taking the focus off our own suffering and pouring out all the empathy, patience, and understanding we gained from our own struggles onto them. In this way, our participation in the body of Christ is critical not only for our own encouragement, but also for the uplifting of others in the body. After all, who else, if not us, can understand the isolation and torment of this disorder? Who else, if not us, can sympathize with other mental struggles, which remain mostly incomprehensible to much of the outside world?

CHAPTER 8

USING THE WORD OF GOD TO DECIPHER GOD'S VOICE

This chapter reviews Scripture that offers the promise of discernment and the ability to distinguish false thinking (including OCD-influenced thoughts) from the truth of God's Word. Because the Bible is infallible and alive, it can help us discern Truth from OCD's lies. We'll look at three passages that armed me with the ability to discern my thoughts. These Scriptures have taught me to both decipher between thoughts caused by OCD and those that are rational—and between thoughts that are motivated by the flesh and those that are inspired by the Holy Spirit living inside me.

Note that I am not saying that different methods of counseling are not biblical ways to seek help; rather, I am saying that all wisdom and direction will ultimately be rooted in the truths found in Scripture.

The Bible Promises That the Word Can Provide Discernment

> We are *destroying speculations and every lofty thing raised up against the knowledge of God, and* we are *taking every thought captive to the obedience of Christ.*
>
> —2 Corinthians 10:5 (NASB 1995)

When I first saw this verse, I immediately focused on "taking every thought captive." However, the first part is equally important in our fight to replace the lies we believe with truth. Paul states that we are to destroy *speculations* and *every lofty thing*. To someone with OCD, this is a very powerful verse because OCD is purely speculation. Thinking that "*if I don't wash my hands, I am going to completely contaminate my entire home*" is mere speculation. Paul is telling us to destroy such speculations.

Paul also speaks of destroying "every lofty thing raised up against the knowledge of God." A lofty thing demands our respect, our deference, and our obedience. In the Bible, lofty things are objects of worship, namely idols. In the example above, the lofty thing is the compulsion to wash one's hands. OCD thoughts demand to be heard and obeyed. However, we have the ability to view our compulsions, no matter how strong they may be, in the same way we would an idol. Once we realize that our compulsions are baseless and that any sense of control we gain by acting on a compulsion is a deception, we can refocus our energy on finding and focusing on thoughts with merit.

The following passages demonstrate how we can use the Word of God as a standard—or litmus test—to which we compare our thoughts.

> *For the word of God is living and powerful, and sharper than any two-edged sword, piercing even to the division of soul and spirit, and of joints and marrow, and is a discerner of the thoughts and intents of the heart.*
>
> —Hebrews 4:12

> *Do not conform any longer to the pattern of this world, but be transformed by the renewing of your mind. Then you will be able to* ***test*** *and approve what God's will is—his good, pleasing and perfect will.*
>
> —Romans 12:2

> *Test all things; hold fast what is good.*
>
> —1 Thessalonians 5:21

> *Beloved, do not believe every spirit, but* ***test*** *the spirits, whether they are of God; because many false prophets have gone out into the world.*
>
> —1 John 4:1

We are commanded to take "every thought captive to the obedience of Christ." Practically speaking, this means we should be aware of our thoughts and whether they line up with the Word of God.

> *Be sober, be vigilant; because your adversary the devil walks about like a roaring lion, seeking whom he may devour. Resist him, steadfast in the faith, knowing that the same sufferings are experienced by your brotherhood in the world.*
>
> —1 Peter 5:8–9

These verses teach us to be consciously aware. For OCD sufferers this includes having an awareness of our thoughts, separate from our emotions, so we can decipher whether they are indeed from God. For all Christians, reality is the truth of God's Word. We can use His Word as an incredible weapon for identifying thoughts that are true and distinguish them from OCD's lies.

Hannah Whitall Smith provides excellent insights:

> It is sometimes thought that the emotions are the governing power in our nature. But I think we all of us know, as a matter of practical experience, that there is something within us, behind our emotions and behind our wishes, an independent self, that, after all, decides everything and controls everything. Our emotions belong to us, and are suffered and enjoyed by us, but they are not ourselves; and if God is to take possession of us, it must be into this central will or personality that He enters. If, then, He is reigning there by the power of His Spirit, all the rest of our nature must come under His sway; and as the will is, so is the man.
>
> The practical bearing of this truth upon the difficulty I am considering is very great. For the decisions of our will are often so directly opposed to the decisions of our emotions, that, if we are in the habit of considering our emotions as the test, we shall be very apt to feel like hypocrites in declaring those things to be real which our will alone has decided. But the moment we see that the will is king, we shall utterly disregard anything that clamors against it, and shall claim as real its decisions, let the emotions rebel as they may."[1]

Years after reading Smith's insights, I was introduced to *Brain Lock* by Jeffrey M. Schwartz, MD, in which he describes the impartial spectator as the "capacity to stand outside your thoughts and watch yourself in action."[2] He claims that people with OCD can use this method to step back from the moment and acknowledge that OCD urges are solely based on a chemical imbalance. Schwartz emphasizes that changing how we respond to this knowledge will change how our brain's function over time.

Schwartz says to ask yourself, "Are my thoughts actual parts of my will and desire, or are they obsessions and compulsions that need to be recognized as such?" He writes, "You must make a conscious effort to keep firmly grounded in reality. You must strive to avoid being tricked into thinking that the feeling that you need to check or to count or to wash, for example, is a real need. It is not.[3]

Schwartz converted from Buddhism to Christianity[4] years after writing this passage, which prescribes one of the leading methods for battling OCD. I find this fascinating, given that his research led him to conclusions that are in line with biblical principles. This correlation is evidenced in the commands to take every thought captive and to think upon worthy things as well as the promise that we are to be transformed by the renewing of our minds.

John Bunyan also realized this truth. After years of condemning thoughts made him think the promises of God might not be for him, he wrote:

> This temptation also helped me put aside my former foolish practice of dismissing the word of promise when it came into my mind. For now, though I could not taste all of the comfort and sweetness from the promise as I had done at other times, I saw that just like a drowning man, I should grab whatever I saw

> that might help me. Previously, I thought I should not carefully consider the promise unless I felt its comfort, but now I could not afford to ignore or reject any hope, as the avenger of blood pursued me so closely.[5]

Although he still considered the condemning thoughts as solely spiritual, Bunyan decided that he could ignore them and cling to the promises of God, whether or not he felt the sweet emotions that should correspond to them.

Now that we know we have the ability to objectively look at our thoughts, it is essential that we cultivate a familiarity with God's character and promises as revealed in the Bible because they provide discernment in even the most confusing mental battles. Consider 2 Timothy 3:14–16:

> *But you must continue in the things which you have learned and been assured of, knowing from whom you have learned them, and that from childhood you have known the Holy Scriptures, which are able to make you wise for salvation through faith which is in Christ Jesus. All Scripture is given by inspiration of God, and is profitable for doctrine, for reproof, for correction, for instruction in righteousness.*

The Bible is the Word of our God, so we must claim these passages as true. The natural progression is to study God's Word and ask Him how His Word can apply in the midst of obsessive, irrational, and controlling thoughts.

As Christians, the standard of what we let into our minds is not only OCD versus not OCD, but what is false versus what aligns with the Truth. The final goal is not only to destroy OCD thoughts, but to destroy all thoughts that are disobedient to how God wants us to think. I propose that we can use God's Word to discern OCD thoughts the same way we use His Word to distinguish the Truth from the lies propagated in a fallen world.

To start, look at the character of God and how it is meant to be reflected in us. We must define how God treats us as His children and how He wants us to think, feel, and react to Him. This will increase our capability for recognizing thoughts and emotions that are from Him versus those that are not. In this section, we will analyze the fruit that the Holy Spirit produces in us (Passage 1), take a close look at what wisdom from God looks like (Passage 2), and end with a reminder of what the fruit of the Spirit of the Law looks like (Passage 3). All these passages are critical to revealing the trademarks of God's gentle voice of Truth versus OCD's harsh and demanding voice of deception.[ix]

Passage 1: Galatians 5:22–23 and the Fruit of the Spirit

Hearing from God while constantly battling obsession, confusion, and condemnation may seem impossible. Although it may be difficult to discern whether a thought is a right thought, seeing its fruit is much easier. For example, if someone didn't know that alcoholism was described as a sin in the Bible, they could still understand it as a negative because it destroys one's career, health, family, and life. The destructive fruit alone is enough of a sign to conclude that alcoholism is not good. In the same way, if thoughts bring the fruit of confusion, condemnation, discouragement, and self-destruction, they cannot be attributed to God. Alternatively, finding thought patterns that allow His fruit to develop helps us decipher which thoughts are coming from Him.

---

ix. OCD led me to make certain that my extrapolations and understanding of these passages were correct. As such, you will notice I have included the Greek words along with the English translation in several instances, which I hope helps strengthen the validity of this chapter.

God gives us a clear list of the fruit that His Holy Spirit produces in us, so we can look at our thoughts and see whether they ultimately lead to the fruit we should expect from a loving Father. Galatians 5:22–23 (NASB 1995) says, *"But the fruit of the Spirit is love, joy, peace, patience, kindness, goodness, faithfulness, gentleness, self-control; against such things there is no law."*

Love

> agapē – *affection* or *benevolence*; specifically, a *love feast:* – (feast of) charity, dear, love[6]

In 1 Corinthians 13:4–8, Paul gives us many descriptions of love, including:

- Love is kind.
- Love is not jealous.
- Love does not brag and is not arrogant.
- Love does not act unbecomingly.
- Love does not seek its own.
- Love is not provoked.
- Love does not take into account a wrong suffered.
- Love believes all things, hopes all things, endures all things.
- Love never fails.

The fruits of OCD are so clearly the opposite of the fruit of the Spirit of God that they are easier to discern than we may think. It's not difficult to discern that OCD-driven thoughts are not loving, especially if we separate ourselves from these thoughts. For the sake of analysis, let's make an exercise of imagining that our OCD thoughts come from an actual person, independent of us. In so doing, let's compare the fruit of OCD's actions to the fruit of love as described above.

- **Love does not seek its own.** OCD commands, "Wash your hands or else the entire building will be contaminated!" Not only does OCD lie to us, but OCD also makes unreasonable demands on us out of its need to control us. OCD demands full compliance, with no exceptions and no mercy, seeking its own will to our detriment—the complete opposite of love!
- **Love is not provoked.** What happens when we do the correct thing and resist giving in to an OCD thought? OCD is provoked in us and increases our anxiety level and tries repeatedly to force us into action. If we dare to argue, push back, or resist, the ugly wrath of OCD rains down on us. OCD practices control, wrath, and punishment—not love.
- **Love never fails.** All OCD does is fail us! The thought, "If I give in to this compulsion, I'll finally be relieved and feel better," is a lie from start to finish. Not only will the relief vanish, but the thought also strengthens itself as we repeat the compulsive acts. OCD demands action with the false promise of protection from pain. In fact, OCD always fails to provide security and to bring the lasting peace and freedom from bondage that love brings.

Joy

chara – *cheerfulness*, that is, calm *delight:* gladness[7]

OCD demands that we perform behaviors in the promise of relief, maybe even joy. In reality, OCD starts with fear, anxiety, and dread, and its demands almost always end in delusion and shame. There is no joy to be had in OCD's demands. In contrast, when God calls us, He gives us the desire to do His will. Although His will and call may seem daunting, He usually gives us joy and gladness to follow His call.

I vividly remember listening to a tape about forgiveness and making things right with others. As I listened, it was clear I should make the difficult decision to reconcile an issue with my dad. Although it was going to be difficult, the idea literally gave me joy. Other times, I've felt that I should reconcile an issue and was driven by guilt and anxiety to apologize. The urge to act seemed so right and even holy, but afterward, I was left with more confusion, anxiety, and even shame. The fruits in this case are the hallmarks of OCD, not the Spirit. In all these instances, I was trying to assuage my relentless thoughts. We can distinguish the gentle call of our loving God, studded with joy and peace, from the harsh and dreadful demands of OCD. Even Hebrews 12:2 says that Christ endured the cross for the joy that was set before Him. Despite the incredible weight of His crucifixion and separation from His Father, joy was before Him. Jesus said in Matthew 11:30, *"For My yoke is easy and My burden is light."* I am convinced that the burden is light, in part, because He works in us to do the things He wants us to do, and He gives us joy in the doing.

Peace

> *eirēnē – Probably from a primary verb eirō (to join); peace (literally or figuratively); by implication prosperity: – one, peace, quietness, rest, and set at one again*[8]

As previously mentioned, I spent much time in college fearing that I might offend someone. When that wasn't the case, I was often feeling guilty for not witnessing to someone or trying to start conversations in the hopes they would lead to discussions about God.

Shortly before my last year of college, I felt called to move into a disgusting, all-male freshman dorm. The building was not air-conditioned, and it was notorious for being a wild place. As the deadline for turning in our room assignments drew near, I specifically prayed about the matter in one of the study rooms in my building. Looking up during my prayer time, I stared out a window that faced the freshman dorm and felt a very distinct peace and even excitement about moving there. My experience was so different from other torturous thoughts I had about witnessing. The decision was not full of anxiety or guilt and didn't even feel like it was something I *had* to do. It had become something I wanted to do. This is a primary difference between OCD and the Holy Spirit. When God's Spirit calls us to action, He does not do it through forced entry into our will. Rather, He literally changes our will to be in line with His! And as a result, peace abounded. Had there been a high level of anxiety or the sense of guilt that I *should be* moving or that I *had to* move, I likely would have rightfully ignored it.

So, when a thought is accompanied by guilt, dread, and the sense of "I have to do this or else," it can be confidently ignored. It should be recognized as not from God. We can rest assured that if we incorrectly ignore a thought, God is gentle, kind, and incredibly patient. He will continue to work on us. God changed my heart. He didn't force me into action through fear of consequences, and He will do the same even if I make a decision in error.

Patience

> makrothumia – (objectively) *forbearance* or (subjectively) *fortitude:* – longsuffering, patience[9]

When comparing patience with the fruit OCD leaves behind, the contrast is obvious. OCD's middle name is literally "Compulsive." Compulsive actions are never based in patience. They demand to be done immediately. When God called me to the freshmen dorm, He took weeks to patiently change my heart to actually desire the move. He did not say, "Fill out your application to move to that disgusting dorm this very second or everyone living there will go to hell!" That would have been impatient and would have caused me to be impatient about my decision as well.

When a thought pressures you into doing something immediately and is full of the fear of consequences, condemnation and guilt, you should confidently attribute it to OCD. Our God is patient; OCD is not. The contrast is stunning.

Kindness

> chrēstotēs – *usefulness*, that is, moral *excellence* (in character or demeanor): – gentleness, goodness[10]

One of my favorite verses in the Bible is Romans 2:4 (NASB 1995), which says, "*Or do you think lightly of the riches of His kindness and tolerance and patience, not knowing that* ***the kindness of God leads you to repentance?***" (emphasis added).

I often find myself acting on a compulsion out of a twisted obligation to repent. This feeling is usually drawn out of a sense of fear or condemnation. Can you think of a time you gave into an OCD thought because it felt like you were led to it by a kind and gentle voice? I certainly can't! When we feel the urge to act because of a harsh, "do-it-now or else!" emotion, we are forgetting how God speaks to His children. He is infinitely kind, and even when we are in sin, His kindness is what leads us to repent, not His wrath or control.

Goodness

> agathōsunē – *goodness*, that is, *virtue* or *beneficence*[11]

I vividly recall the moment my daughter was born. She was so precious, pure, and gentle. She did not have an ounce of guile, deceit, arrogance, malice, or contempt. She simply trusted and existed. The character of children is one aspect of God's goodness He has let us see in creation. After all, children are created in His image and have yet to be influenced by this sinful world.

Creation itself is also a place to see goodness: a sunrise on the beach, a meadow in the calm of a huge expanse of land, and the beauty and diversity of the animal kingdom all clearly scream of the goodness of our Creator. When I have felt God's presence strongly, two things were made overwhelmingly obvious to my soul. The first was that He is holy, and I am not. I was completely unworthy to be in His presence and deserved only rejection from Him. The second was that God is as loving, merciful, and gracious toward me as He is holy. His presence gave me an immeasurable sense of belonging, acceptance, and redemption in my feeble flesh. That feeling is truly indescribable. And from that experience alone, I knew God was good. It wasn't that He was either Holy or merciful; it was that He was somehow both at an incalculable degree all at the same time.

Our flesh often bends our understanding of who God is to one side of His character or the other. Either we see His grace as permissiveness and want to take advantage of it by sinning, or we see His holiness and are immobilized by the condemnation of our sin. The true character of God, however, shows us both truths simultaneously and leads us to love God because He is good.

I know for a fact that God is merciful and patient and understanding. And although He is holy and demands holiness, He is also gentle and kind. This is something we are to experience moment by moment because the requirement of our holiness has been perfectly fulfilled by Christ (see Matthew 5:17). I am convinced that this inexplicably gracious fulfillment of His demand for holiness is a part of what makes Him good. So when OCD attacks and makes you feel like you must "do something, and do it now or else!," it shows itself separate from the mercy, gentleness, or kindness that a thought from God would have.

Faithfulness

> pistis – *persuasion*, that is, *credence*; moral *conviction* (of *religious* truth, or the truthfulness of God or a religious teacher), especially *reliance* upon Christ for salvation; abstract *constancy* in such profession; by extension the system of religious (Gospel) *truth* itself: – assurance, belief, believe, faith, fidelity[12]

In 2 Timothy 2:13, Paul says, *"If we are faithless, He remains faithful; He cannot deny Himself."* Faithfulness is possibly the most important attribute of God for OCD sufferers to focus and lean on. His faithfulness in the midst of our unfaithfulness goes against all we see in the world. The translation of the Hebrew word *pistis* includes the idea of "reliance upon Christ for salvation." The natural response to a faithful God is reliance on Him. OCD thoughts force us to rely on ourselves, our own behaviors, and our own abilities to control circumstances or perform a compulsive action properly. God never gives us thoughts or rituals that overwhelm us or force us to depend on ourselves, lest a terrible consequence befall us. God's faithfulness means we don't have to be in control and that we can fully rely on Him.

Self-Control

> egkrateia – *self-control* (especially *continence*): – temperance[13]

OCD manifests itself when our self-control is overcome and we comply with the urge to perform a compulsion. For instance, when the idea of having to wash our hands overtakes us so completely that we give in to washing, we have been coerced and are not exercising self-control over our own thoughts, emotions, or behaviors. A thought from God would never beat down our self-control and *force* us into a behavior we can't resist based on anxiety and a fear of negative consequences. As OCD sufferers, it is important to be conscious of our self-will so that we can recognize when our will is not in line with the compulsions. The Holy Spirit ministers to our hearts and gently teaches us the ways of God, urging our self-will to act in obedience out of love for God—all for our blessing. OCD attempts to beat our self-will into obedience through fear and anxiety.

Passage 2: James 3:17 and Wisdom from Above

I am sometimes terrified by the fear of deception. In the past, I occasionally attributed a specific thought from God to my sinful flesh. Worse, I credited the thought to Satan, fearing I had committed a terrible sin. Conversely, I feared that if I attributed a tempting thought, or worse yet one from Satan, to God, I would end up deceived and far from God's presence. This is just one example, but OCD sufferers face many variations of this on a daily basis. At the crux is the basic question: How do I distinguish the wisdom of God from the lies that OCD tells? This is where James 3:17 can be used as a tool in battling these scenarios.

> *But wisdom from above is first pure, then peaceable, gentle, reasonable, full of mercy and good fruit, unwavering, without hypocrisy.*
>
> —James 3:17 (NASB 1995)

Pure

> hagnotēs – *cleanness* (the state), that is blamelessness: – pureness[14]

One of the definitions of *pureness* in *Webster's Dictionary* is, "characterized by no appreciable alteration of articulation during utterance."[15] Purity is clear and uncomplicated, much like the purity of fresh spring water versus the putrid mess of swamp water. In terms of human hearts, purity includes the absence of ulterior and selfish motives.

The hallmarks of OCD thoughts are their lack of clarity and the complicated and opaque reasoning behind them. OCD thoughts deceive and have their own ulterior motive: control. OCD is never satisfied because it demands perfection. OCD demands always lead to more demands, repetition of the same demand, or a lack of clarity regarding what to do next. OCD compulsions promise relief, but relief is rarely, if ever, truly realized.

When you take a thought captive, test whether it is complicated and murky, lacks clarity, makes elusive promises, or proves untrue. Does it leave you unsettled and confused or bring you true peace? Do you have to jump through 100 hoops to get to the end result? Do the things you feel you *need* to do make little sense in reality? If so, they are impure—not in the sense of being sinful; rather, they are not simple, logical, or direct in their meaning. Even when God asked people to do extravagant things in the Bible, it was never confusing. Rather, the instructions were clear and easy to understand.

I have had the pleasure of seeing how well my grandfather understood the meaning of purity in this verse. He lived a life of faith for many decades, and it astounded me how obvious he found God's will. I had hundreds of conversations with him, and not once did he ever hint that God's will was a difficult or mysterious thing for him to grasp. He simply knew God was good and did what was right. His faith in God's goodness made him confident that his simple approach to decision-making would be blessed because God looks at the heart and not our ability to de-code some mysterious path we think He wants us to take. His ways are pure and uncomplicated, unlike our own. And very much unlike the thought patterns born from OCD.

Peaceable

> eirēnikos – *pacific*; by implication *salutary:* – peaceable[16]

Webster's defines *salutary* as "producing a beneficial effect."[17] Second, it defines *peaceable* as "not contentious or quarrelsome, quietly behaved, and free from strife or disorder."[18] Thoughts leading to compulsion do not produce a beneficial effect and are instead full of strife and disorder. OCD is incredibly contentious and creates strife by making us miserable until we perform a compulsion. After we do it, we don't feel good about it. And often, it leads to strife between us and others who get in OCD's way. OCD promises to bring us peace through compulsive actions but never fulfills that promise. OCD thoughts are not born of peace, but of all forms of anxiety and fear. Put simply, OCD thoughts lead to actions that destroy our peace and that of those around us.

Gentle

> epieikēs – *appropriate*, that is, (by implication) *mild:* – gentle, moderation, patient[19]

OCD thoughts are loud, demanding, and induce action through the fear of dire consequences. There is nothing gentle about these thoughts. The feelings associated with them are severe, and often the thoughts themselves are severe. They convince us that if we do not perform an action, we or someone else will suffer a drastic consequence. The consequence is rarely (if ever) moderate, small, or reasonable. I doubt anyone has ever had the OCD thought, "Wash your hands or you'll have to stay at work for 10 extra seconds today!" Rather, the thoughts use the fear of a dire consequence to manipulate us into action. So, if you feel inclined to give in to a thought, ask yourself, "Will I be happy about giving in to this action?" Notice that *giving in* implies that force is being used to bring the result. God kindly and gently leads us in the ways we should repent. When God wants us to do something, He calls us in gentleness. When God speaks to us, even when it is to expose our sins to us so that we realize our complete inability to be holy as He is, He is kind and gentle. Force and conflict are not how He communicates with us.

Reasonable

> eupeithēs – *good for persuasion*, that is, (intransitively) compliant*:* – easy to be intreated[20]

Webster's definition of *reasonable* could also be "the opposite of an OCD thought." We never look back at an OCD thought to which we submitted and say, "Wow, I am sure glad I did that," because the thought was not reasonable to begin with. This is why we are often embarrassed and hide our compulsive actions from those around us. We fear they might think we are crazy or at least that they wouldn't understand.

If a thought is unreasonable, it isn't from God. I am not ignoring all the times that God used people in the Bible to do His will through what we see as very unreasonable actions (e.g., all the stories of faith mentioned in Hebrews 11, such as Noah building an ark during a long drought). However, note that in all these instances, God spoke very clearly and directly to these people.

I feel that God has given me the gift of evangelism, and I have sometimes felt encouraged and excited to lead a particular conversation toward matters of faith. However, at other times I've felt consumed and overwhelmed by guilt and anxiety for not seizing opportunities to evangelize, such as helping someone with a flat tire or giving food to a homeless person outside a convenience store. So, although it takes courage and sometimes seems daunting to evangelize, God does not call us to evangelism through guilt, fear, and anxiety. Rather, He gives us the desire and provides the opportunity.

When God asks us to do something we think is unreasonable, He prepares us in terms of strength of faith. There may be nervous moments, as stepping out in faith is a potentially scary thing, but the feelings will not be accompanied by irrationality and overwhelmingly negative emotions. So, if I go a long period without evangelizing, I have oftentimes prayed that God would show me opportunities to do so. Usually, within a week or two, I find myself speaking to someone about Him in a natural and unforced way.

So, when I'm unable to discern whether God wants me to do something, I am learning to focus on truths I *know*. God's thoughts and His will for me are reasonable. When guilt creeps in while I'm obsessing over the chance God wants me to do something, I focus on His goodness as a Shepherd and all the other fruit of the Spirit to help me better discern God's voice. If I miss an opportunity, I have a loving Father who will guide me to make better choices in the future.

Full of Mercy

> eleos – Of uncertain affinity; *compassion* (human or divine, especially active): – (+ tender) mercy[21]

OCD is *not* merciful. It is consuming, relentless, and destructive. Nothing about it is merciful, let alone full of mercy. Any passing thought that says, "do this or the world will end, or you will go to hell, or your loved ones will be in harm's way," is not merciful and should be immediately ignored.

OCD is unforgiving in its demands, showing no mercy no matter how much we might suffer, nor how faithfully we have bowed down to its compulsions. In contrast, God's mercy is offered to us when we need it the most—when we have sinned and fallen short, when we have been imperfect, and when we are suffering the consequences of those behaviors.

Note that I am not speaking of gross sin that God's Word clearly describes. For example, we should be extreme in avoiding sins such as lust, murder, and adultery because the earthly consequences are great, and those sins keep us far from God. However, if a thought leads you to an action that has no place in God's Word—such as washing your hands for the twentieth time today to prevent some horrible consequence from taking place, we can know it is not from God.

Unwavering

adiakritos – *impartial:* – without partiality[22]

OCD thoughts waver and change their demands from moment to moment, as in the case of the person who has to go home to check and recheck whether the door is locked before heading to work. At what point is rechecking enough? After two times? Five times? Ten times? And if there is a number, why does it change? Why does checking become unbearable one day, an afterthought the next, or even disappear altogether?

The answer is that OCD does not follow any rules. It has no consistent level of demand. It simply wreaks havoc when and where it wants to and spreads wherever and whenever it can. In contrast, God's Word and character never change. He is the same yesterday, today, and forever. We can find rest in that.

Without Hypocrisy

> anupokritos – *undissemled,* that is, without dissimulation (hypocrisy), unfeigned[23]

Dissimulate means to disguise or conceal under a false appearance.[24] We can use this description as a litmus test by asking ourselves, "Is the appearance of this thought a reflection of reality?" For example, the thought, "you will contaminate the entire city if you don't wash your hands," gives a false appearance. The implication is that the opposite is true—that washing your hands will prevent contamination of the city. But how will repetitively washing my hands help keep things clean when so many other factors can affect my cleanliness, the cleanliness of my surroundings, and the cleanliness of all the people and things in an entire city? The answer is that OCD almost always selects which agenda it wishes to push, implying that a problem can be solved by an action, which is usually unreasonable. In reality, there is rarely a problem at all. In this example, re-washing my hands has no effect on keeping the city uncontaminated. There are millions of other contaminants directly impacting this issue of greater significance than my handwashing. A city is flooded by germs on the ground, bacterial and viral infections in the air, and all manners of filth. Therefore, ask yourself, "Is this thought giving a false appearance of control, and second, is it presenting a nonexistent problem to begin with?"

Passage 3: 2 Corinthians 3:6 and the Spirit of the Law

The great gift of Christ to all mankind is liberation from the letter of the Law, which kills. The letter of the Law demands perfection, which humans cannot—even with much striving—achieve. But as OCD sufferers, we can live under this kind of demand for perfection on a daily, hourly, or moment-by-moment basis. Does this kind of slavery that kills sound like your thought life? As children of a gracious and loving God, we need to remember that we live under the Spirit of the Law that brings life, not the letter that kills.

> *Not that we are adequate in ourselves to consider anything as coming from ourselves, but our adequacy is from God, who also made us adequate as servants of a new covenant, not of the letter but of the Spirit; for the letter kills, but the Spirit gives life.*
>
> —2 Corinthians 3:5–6 (NASB 1995)

> *But he is a Jew who is one inwardly; and circumcision is that which is of the heart, by the Spirit, not by the letter; and his praise is not from men, but from God.*
>
> —Romans 2:29 (NASB 1995)

> *Therefore you are no longer a slave but a son, and if a son, then an heir of God through Christ.*
>
> —Galatians 4:7

OCD demands perfect compliance to its own "letter of the law." Our compulsive thoughts compel us to do something very specific and very perfectly to satisfy OCD. It may or may not be the letter of the Law from the Bible, but in both cases, the result is not freedom. If the God of the universe has liberated us from the letter of the law that kills, how is OCD justified in enslaving us?

A common pattern experienced by believers with OCD is to question their own salvation. Of course, this can manifest in many forms, but let's take a look at how an OCD sufferer might wrestle with John 3:16:

> *For God so loved the world that He gave His only begotten Son, that whoever believes in Him should not perish but have everlasting life.*

The intention of this verse is to demonstrate the overwhelming mercy of God and the hope He brings by promising eternal life to those who are spiritually dead. This ultimately leads to life in the Spirit as 2 Corinthians 3:5–6 promises.

Instead of appreciating that this promise is freely given, fulfilled, and sealed by God for eternity regardless of our limitations and failures, OCD sufferers often turn the responsibility for being eligible for the promise back on themselves. This is done through thoughts such as: *"Oh no, what if I don't believe? How can I know for sure that I am a Christian? What if I think I believe but I really don't?"*

Inevitably, this results in trying to figure out exactly what it means to believe or trying to test our emotions to ensure they are real. This anxiety leads to compulsion, and we often end up saying, "OK, just to make sure I'm a Christian I'll re-pray the sinner's prayer again or read a book on what it means to really pray."

By doing this, we take the law of the Spirit (freedom from duty and reliance on God) and turn it into our own letter of the law (burden and reliance on our performance). Thus, the verse, which screamed of God's *unmerited* gift of love, becomes a laundry list of things we need to do to "make sure" we know we believe. When that happens, we need to look at the fruit of the Spirit and the description of wisdom from above. When we do that, we can see whether we are drifting into the slavery of the letter of the law instead of basking in the freedom and joy of the Spirit of the new covenant.

When You Are Desperate, Call Out to Your Abba, Father

God knows how to meet us in our desperation. When Christ called out to God in the Garden of Gethsemane, He used the phrase *"Abba, Father!"* (Mark 14:36). As children of God, we too can call out to God in this way. Romans 8:15 states that we have *"received the Spirit of adoption"* and are to use the same phrase as Christ did. Furthermore, *"Abba, Father"* is used again in Galatians 4:6, which promises that we have the Holy Spirit. He has said, *"I will never leave you nor forsake you"* (Hebrews 13:5). The *Bible Knowledge Commentary* states:

> The word *Abba* is the Aramaic word for "Father." It is the diminutive form used by small children in addressing their fathers. It is appropriate to see the similarity to the English word "Daddy." Used by Christ (cf. Mark 14:36), *this familiar form indicates intimacy and trust as opposed to the formalism of legalism.* (emphasis added)[25]

Will God ever discipline His children? Absolutely. But don't confuse His loving discipline with that of a harsh master who so easily disregards the well-being of his servants. So, take captive any thought that demeans you, condemns you, or treats you in a way that a perfect father wouldn't—and get rid of it. Ask yourself: "Does the thought *clearly* lead me to become more like Christ? Or is it confusing, burdensome and dreadful?"

God does not intend for us to carry the burden of OCD alone, and He definitely doesn't beat us down with it. Christ Himself intercedes for us, and God takes care of us more than we know. He knows our frailty and inabilities, so we can cling to His promises with confidence. Remember that God is greater than our hearts:

> *My little children, let us not love in word or in tongue, but in deed and in truth. And by this we know that we are of the truth, and shall assure our hearts before Him. For if our heart condemns us, God is greater than our heart, and knows all things.*
>
> —1 John 3:18–20

When feelings of condemnation overwhelm us and we feel like God's voice is a million miles away, God is greater than our hearts, and He knows all things. Even if we feel like we have betrayed or blasphemed Him a million times, He knows our hearts more than we ever will. He knows the intentions we have to remain near Him and obey Him. His grace will carry us and cover us.[x]

---

x. I recommend copying the verses from this chapter onto index cards (or adding them as notes on a smartphone) and reviewing them whenever needed. This suggestion also applies to the Scripture verses found throughout this book.

CHAPTER 9

OCD'S KRYPTONITE – THE ATMOSPHERE OF GOD'S GRACE

As most people know, Kryptonite was a foreign mineral that had the property of depriving Superman of his power. In the same way, OCD is deprived of its power when we celebrate and cling to the great privilege of freedom we have, living under the protection of God's grace. Put another way, OCD cannot thrive where grace is present. In this chapter we will contrast the atmosphere of God's grace with the atmosphere of legalism, to reveal why God's grace is the key to triumph over OCD's power. John 1:5 states, "*The light shines in the darkness, and the darkness has not overcome it*" (NIV). In the same way, I am convinced that grace shines on us in the midst of our OCD, and OCD cannot overcome grace!

Legalism and OCD

In my Christian experience, OCD often sucks me into legalism. In *The Grace of God*, Tony Evans describes how legalism can impact our motivations:

- "Legalism is trying to please God 'by the flesh,' by attempting to keep a list of laws and rules we think will earn us God's favor and keep us in good standing with Him. It is identity based on performance rather than relationship. It makes rule-keeping the basis of spiritual victory."[1]
- "Grace-based Christians obey because it's their delight. Law-based Christians obey because it's their duty. Grace-based Christians obey and love it. Law-based Christians obey and resent it."[2]
- "Legalism puts people under an impossible load. Who could possibly keep the whole law? One consequence of legalism is the joyless bondage of trying harder, yet continually falling short."[3]

When I initially read these statements, I could not help noticing that living under the burden of legalism and living with OCD can be described almost identically. Our propensity toward legalism is constantly fueled by the cycle of obsession (fear) followed by the drive to compulsion (works), echoing Dr. Evans's conclusion that people end up with the "joyless bondage of trying harder, yet continually falling short."

The Atmosphere Created by Legalism

Imagine having the worst boss in the world. He is well known for his ruthlessness, cruelty, short fuse, lack of empathy, and propensity to be harsh toward his employees. Despite this, suppose he makes a grand promise to you. He claims he'll promote you and give you a 25% raise if you get a satisfactory review at year-end. Because of the nature of his character, you would find any and all reasons not to trust him. You would likely become obsessed with never getting caught doing something that might allow him to void his promise, no matter how small. You would second-guess your decision-making, work, and level of effort. Your anxiety would grow as you saw the risk of slipping up in every situation and being disqualified from the promotion. You may even beat yourself up for every tiny mistake and minor error, knowing how harsh and ruthless your review would be. Working daily in dread would become normal, and in your heart, you would begin to despise your boss.

OCD sufferers are familiar with this atmosphere because OCD treats us the way a cruel master would. If grace is unmerited favor, then I would describe OCD as unmerited condemnation. And the resulting environment can seep into our relationship with God in the form of legalism. This wreaks havoc on our attempts to be joyful in the Lord, have peace, and confidently approach God in prayer.

This is why one of the biggest tests OCD sufferers face is believing that God is as good and gracious toward them as He says He is. I believe the most powerful way to fight this oppressive atmosphere is by believing in His promise of *grace*.

Grace Defined

Grace is commonly defined as undeserved favor. Dr. Evans defines grace as:

> The inexhaustible supply of God's goodness whereby He does for us what we could never do for ourselves, what we do not deserve, what we cannot earn and

> what we never could repay. It is what God does for us INDEPENDENT of us. Grace emanates from God to us WITHOUT us. It is a whole new world of operating, and it is a world that does not come natural to us.[4]

This is good news for all Christians—especially sweet to those with OCD. Since it's undeserved and independent of us, no compulsions are required. OCD harshly commands us to fear dire consequences if we don't act on compulsions, and it only offers temporary relief when we succumb to its demands. Conversely, when we fully lean on God's grace, we realize there are no cruel or harsh requirements for being intimate and right with God. His grace is undeserved, and it is free.

I've spent decades struggling to experience God's grace. Once, I was so desperate I followed a preacher to his car just after he preached to pick his brain about love and grace. I asked him how to experience grace when I constantly feared I might be in sin. He described God's grace like standing under a powerful shower. Dirt may get on us from time to time, but it is removed instantly by the powerful stream of clean water. Even if I was getting dirty and didn't know it, the water would clean me off.

Now that I have a child, I am able to comprehend the meaning of grace in my heart more than ever before. The moment my daughter was born, she had all my favor, and it was unmerited because she had accomplished absolutely nothing and had done nothing for me. The same is true for us. Remember Romans 8:15 and how we are adopted children of our Abba, Father. When my child calls for daddy, I feel joy and want nothing more than to hear what she has to say. This is how God feels about us and responds to us.

The New Environment of Grace

Recall the example of the tyrannical boss. As unhealthy and terrible as that work environment would be, over time it would begin to feel normal. It is no different with OCD. It becomes our normal operating environment.

In his sermon "The Concept of Grace," Dr. Evans describes grace as an atmosphere in which we live and move and function. He says that grace is like soil: in the same way a vegetable grows out of soil, we are to grow out of the soil of grace.[5]

Although God deals with us under the covenant of grace, many Christians operate in the old covenant (the law) and don't experientially transfer to the new covenant of grace. They are stuck in a system that God is no longer operating in. Evans explains, "If your Christian life is miserable even though you want to see victory, then you need to understand grace because it is God's liberating word."[6] Evans adds that "Grace is like moving to a new culture. Someone who does so would have to learn a new language and get used to the freedoms granted to all in the new country. BUT IT IS NOT NATURAL, and one would have to get used to it."[7]

Evans points out that "Grace gives us victory and is the mechanism for peace, the mechanism for joy and the mechanism for power."[8] As such, we have to get unstuck from thinking in terms of the old covenant and start thinking in terms of the new covenant.[9]

The good news is that "Grace is ALWAYS FREE, there are no strings attached (Romans 3:24, Revelation 21:6, and 22:13). Grace is powerful.[10] Romans 5:20 states that the law came in so that transgressions would increase. The law is the covenant of condemnation. All the law does is show you how sinful you are; it cannot help you get better. But where sin increased, grace abounded all the more. Grace does what the law could never do. Finally, Evans declares, "Grace delivers us from sin, the law has no power to do so. To have victory we need more grace, not more effort."[11]

How to Walk in the Environment of Grace

God's grace by definition is *undeserved* favor, meaning it is favor from God *independent* of anything we have done, do, or could ever do to earn it or lose it. This truth welcomes us into an atmosphere that is sweet, full of peace, rest, and joy. On the other hand, OCD regularly drags us into the exact opposite atmosphere with one overarching lie—that the weight of virtually everything we worry about is *our responsibility alone*. Grace leads us to continually lean on God and transfer responsibility to Him, for it is His grace that sustains us and keeps us safe.

In *Can Christianity Cure Obsessive-Compulsive Disorder?*, Ian Osborn, MD, gives far more insight into this issue. He says that multiple giants of the Christian faith found a form of therapy that "rests on the pillar of truth that is repeatedly emphasized in both the Old Testament and in the Gospels: All that is needed is unconditional trust in God."[12]

As we learn to walk in this trust, we will be transformed by the renewing of our minds (Romans 12:2). In light of Romans 12:2, it is no surprise that Dr. Schwartz concludes that we can learn to revalue thoughts. "With consistent practice, you will quickly come to realize that your obsessive thoughts and compulsive behaviors are worthless distractions to be ignored."[13]

The Environment of Grace and the Ability to Take Risks

Let's flip the story of the cruel boss in our example. Let's assume he is a man full of grace toward his employees. I actually had a boss like that. His name was Kenn, and he was my first boss after college. He constantly built up his employees, allowed them to grow, publicly praised them when they succeeded, and once presented an award to an intern in front of the CEO of our multi-billion dollar company.

Nobody tried to take advantage of the gracious atmosphere he had created. In fact, most of those reporting to him were inspired to give their absolute best. And what was the result? That intern became my colleague and was eventually promoted to general manager at one of our larger sites.

To borrow again from Dr. Evans, Kenn planted us in good soil that allowed us to grow. The key here is that his grace allowed me and my coworkers to try new things, take risks, and sometimes fail. We freely took risks because we knew our boss was intent on bettering the company and would be full of grace if a mistake was made.

And this is the standard for whether we are growing in the environment of grace: We are beating this disorder when we start making decisions based on God's grace, not on fear of negative consequences.

My brother is an inventor and blew me away once with how this concept is ingrained upon his soul. He was asked to give a graduation speech and requested that he be allowed to speak about God. When I asked him what he would say, without hesitating, he matter of factly replied:

> Well, I see my relationship with God as similar to a child in a sandbox. My loving father is sitting right next to me watching me make things. If I make a castle that looks ugly, He doesn't get mad or even say anything. I can just start over. All that interests my dad is that I'm secure in His love and that I'm using my creativity to have joy with Him.

This is the picture of God He wants us to have. He looks at us and sees the perfection of Christ. He wants us to understand that His love for us is greater than any love we could ever feel or give. His Word says so. The hope provided by God and the field of psychiatry is this: the more you combat OCD, the smaller it becomes in your life. My hope is that this book helps lead you into the new atmosphere of relying on God and seeing His never-ending grace toward you— *independent of your performance.* The Bible's constant theme is about relying on Christ's work on the cross for salvation, the Holy Spirit in us to secure that salvation, and on the Father's love toward us, which points us to the same truth. There is nothing we can do to earn God's favor, yet we have it because He has shown us favor *independent* of anything we have done or could do. And the more baby steps we take toward that truth, the closer we are to making huge strides toward victory over OCD.

CHAPTER 10

RECOMMENDED READING AND LISTENING

I commend to you several resources by authors who have brilliantly linked Scriptural truth with therapy for OCD:

Crawford, Mark. *The Obsessive-Compulsive Trap: Real Help for a Real Struggle.* Ventura, CA: Regal Books, 2004. Mark Crawford has an MS and a PhD in clinical psychology and is an outspoken Christian.

Emlet, Michael R. *OCD: Freedom for the Obsessive-Compulsive.* Phillipsburg, NJ: P&R Publishing Company, 2004. Dr. Emlet holds MD and MDiv degrees and is a faculty member at the Christian Counseling and Educational Foundation. His extensive medical and theological education coupled with many years of practical counseling experience make this book rare and invaluable.

Osborn, Ian. *Can Christianity Cure Obsessive-Compulsive Disorder?: A Psychiatrist Explores the Role of Faith in Treatment.* Grand Rapids, MI: Brazos Press, 2008. This book gives excellent insight into how we can learn to constantly rely on God through this disorder. Osborn is not only a psychiatrist, but he also has OCD, which gives him invaluable insight and wisdom.

Osborn, Ian. *Tormenting Thoughts and Secret Rituals: The Hidden Epidemic of Obsessive-Compulsive Disorder.* New York: Dell Publishing, 1998. This work explains the nature of OCD and reviews causes and treatments for OCD. Osborn's research into how OCD has been treated historically is fascinating and unparalleled.

Schwartz, Jeffrey M. with Beverly Beyette. *Brain Lock: A Four-Step Self-Treatment Method to Change Your Brain Chemistry.* New York: HarperCollins Publishers, Inc., 1996. Schwartz is an MD, a psychiatrist, and one of the leading OCD experts in the US. His groundbreaking four-step method lines up with biblical principles, and Schwartz converted to Christianity years after writing the book. His proposed method is one of the most successful on record.

VanCleve, Mitzi. *Strivings Within – The OCD Christian: Overcoming Doubt and Anxiety in the Storm of Anxiety.* Self-pub, Createspace Independent Publishing Platform, 2015. VanCleve not only has OCD, but has also struggled from social anxiety and panic attacks.

Wells, Jeff. *Breaking Free of OCD: My Battle with Mental Pain and How God Rescued Me.* Houston, TX: Lucid Books, 2016. Aside from being a world-class marathon runner, Jeff holds both a Master of Theology and a Doctor of Ministry from Dallas Theological Seminary. Despite such a rigorous educational background in the Bible, his struggle with OCD should help OCD doubters see that this disorder is more than just spiritual or a lack of knowing God's promises.

Additional Resources

Bunyan, John. *Grace Abounding to the Chief of Sinners.* Abbotsford, WI: Aneko Press, 2017. This book was written in the seventeenth century, yet I doubt any current-day OCD sufferer could read his words and deny that Bunyan struggled with the disorder. This book is a great example of how OCD can wreak havoc on the spiritual life of a Christian. Twelve years after its publication, Bunyan published the first part of the classic *The Pilgrim's Progress,* which has over 1,300 editions in print. I recommend the most recent translation for ease of reading.

Evans, Tony. "The Grace of God" based on his 12-part sermon series titled, "The Magnificent Grace of God." Although Dr. Evans did not create this series specifically for OCD sufferers, I have found it to be incredibly liberating because OCD and legalism are very similar. I have listened to each of the sermons multiple times. This series a powerful tool because grace is such a foreign experience and concept for OCD sufferers.

Landsman, Karen, Kathleen M. Parrish, and Cherlene Pedrick. *Loving Someone with OCD: Help for You and Your Family.* Oakland, CA: New Harbinger Publications, 2005.

Spurgeon, Charles. *Being God's Friend.* New Kensington, PA: Whitaker House, 1997. Spurgeon is known as the "Prince of Preachers."

APPENDIX

This appendix is for those of you who do not identify as a Christian but may be reading this book to help a Christian friend, relative, child, or possibly even a patient. The appendix presents a brief explanation of the promises that Christianity gives to its followers. Whether you believe them or not, I hope you agree that the following love story is the most amazing one ever told.

The Chief and the Thief

One of the best analogies I've ever heard regarding the story of Christianity was during a sermon by Pastor Steve King at Cherrydale Baptist Church in Arlington, Virginia.[1] The story is about an Indian Chief who was well-respected by his tribe for being full of both justice and love. One day, some elder tribesmen came to the chief and explained that there was significant thievery occurring within the community. Since the chief was all about justice, he decreed that the punishment for the thief would involve being tied to a post and lashed to death.

Eventually, the thief was caught and brought before the chief who was horrified to learn that the thief was none other than his one and only son. What was he to do? On one hand, he was all about justice, so he couldn't just let it slide. Anything less than following through on what was decreed would make his word less than honorable. On the other hand, lashing his son to death was unimaginable to him.

Then came the day of judgment. The chief watched as the elder in charge of the lashings began to prepare his whip, while others tied the chief's son to a post. Moments before the first lash was given, the chief yelled, "Wait!" Many in the crowd thought they knew what was about to happen. They suspected that the chief's love for his son had finally outweighed his resolve for justice. Maybe he would make his son a servant to those from whom he had stolen. Or would he lessen the severity of the lashing so the son would survive? Or would he make him work wretched jobs until he repaid all that he had stolen?

But no, the chief truly was about justice, and nothing less than death would be a just punishment, for that is what he had decreed. He said nothing to the crowd or to his son, but stripped off his shirt and wrapped his body around his son's, so his body would receive the deadly lashes and protect his son from certain death.

The crowd watched in astonishment as the elder lashed the chief to death. He never wavered and never tried to use his power and influence to change what had to be done. Upon his death, the tribe knew he was truly the type of man he claimed to be—one full of both justice and love.

Jesus and Mankind

This story is an excellent analogy of the gospel of Jesus Christ. We humans represent the thieving son, while the chief represents God and His holiness and love.

One of the biggest temptations for us is to think that we are sufficient enough to stand before God on our own. It's very easy to conclude we are good by comparing ourselves to others, or by thinking that our good actions outweigh our bad ones. The issue is that when we do that, we use our own standard of goodness and righteousness. God's standard requires perfect holiness—something none of us can attain. Romans 3:23 says, "*for all have sinned and fall short of the glory of God.*"

The consequence of missing the mark is the same as the consequence in the story above. Romans 6:23 says, "*For the wages of sin* is *death, but the gift of God* is *eternal life in Christ Jesus our Lord*" (emphasis added). Because God is perfectly just, the payment for sin must be made with a perfect sacrifice. That is why Christ is the only path to God the Father. In John 14:6, Jesus says, "*I am the way, the truth, and the life. No one comes to the Father except through Me.*" We can't work our way back into good standing with God. Before Christ, the only way the Jewish people could remain in good standing with God was to offer unblemished blood sacrifices year after year.

God wanted to be with us forever, but we had chosen sin, and His holiness demanded perfection. The only solution was a perfect sacrifice, namely His perfect Son. So, God sent His Son to earth in the form of a man.

Matthew 1:20–21 states that an angel came and spoke to Joseph saying:

> *Joseph, son of David, do not be afraid to take to you Mary your wife, for that which is conceived in her is of the Holy Spirit. And she will bring forth a Son, and you shall call His name Jesus, for He will save His people from their sins.*

When Christ came to earth, He was fully man and also fully God. He was the ultimate and final sacrifice. He died in our place just as the chief died for his son.

In Matthew 27:46, Jesus cried out, *"My God, My God, why have You forsaken Me?"* as he hung on the cross and died. His intense agony was not just from the nails that held Him to the cross or the suffocation involved in the crucifixion process. Infinitely more agonizing was His separation from His Father as He took the payment for all mankind's sin upon Himself.

Christ's death is the greatest love story ever told. But it didn't end there. He overcame death and rose from the dead three days later (Mark 16, Luke 24, Romans 6, Romans 8, and 1 Corinthians 15). (There is an abundance of evidence surrounding this historical event in *The Case for Christ*[2] and *The Case for the Resurrection,* [3]both by author Lee Strobel.)

Salvation is free and available to anyone who believes in His payment for and power over sin. John 3:16–17 states:

> *For God so loved the world that He gave His only begotten Son, that whoever believes in Him should not perish but have everlasting life. For God did not send His Son into the world to condemn the world, but that the world through Him might be saved.*

OCD and the Gospel of Salvation

Faith in the gospel of Jesus Christ is what makes one a Christian. The gift is free and solely based on grace (undeserved favor). It requires no work to be received. As you can see, from an intellectual standpoint, this story is very easy to understand. You may wonder how someone could ever struggle with guilt, condemnation, or fear if they truly believed the gospel message. However, OCD is very creative at inventing worst-case scenarios, then convincing its sufferers that they alone are responsible for preventing those scenarios from coming to fruition. Because of this, such scenarios are worse for Christian OCD sufferers. They involve eternal separation from the God who loves us as much as He promises. Missing out on eternity with Him is a terrifying thought, one that can wreak havoc on our minds.

And it's not just missing out on eternity with God that causes anxiety in a Christian with OCD, but also the fear of ruining their current relationship with God in the here and now. God promises to be with us as we live day by day on earth. OCD constantly works to make us believe we will ruin that daily relationship.

OCD isn't caused by faith in Christ and a God who gives infinite promises. Rather, OCD is amplified by the fact that the worst-case scenario that the OCD sufferer is trying to avoid is infinitely larger than if a loving and eternal God didn't exist. I say this because as a child, I once had an atheist psychiatrist tell me to stop praying and taking my relationship with God so seriously. That was out of place on multiple levels, including the idea that minimizing the role of "religion" in my life would help reduce my OCD symptoms. In contrast, it was my relationship with God—and the strong presence of His grace and mercy—that sustained me during the times when OCD was nearly at its worst. I hope this helps you to bridge the gap of understanding between you and Christian OCD sufferers.

Last, I'm sure the Christians around you would love nothing more than to hear that their friend, parent, or counselor decided to accept God's promises and believe the good news that He has given us. So, if you believe, simply pray: Admit to God that you sin and are in need of forgiveness, that you believe He sent His son Jesus to earth through the virgin Mary, that Jesus died and rose again to pay for and defeat sin, and that you accept Him as your Savior.

It truly is that simple, completely undeserved favor, which is why it is called the Good News. It is utterly opposed to the world's message and even our own natural desires, which live by the rule of an eye for an eye and tend to give affection based on merit and selfish gain.

A religious studies student once raised his hand and asked his professor what makes Christianity so special and unique compared to all the other religions in the world. The professor looked at him and said, "Young man, it can be boiled down to one word, and that word is *grace*. Every other religion is predicated on what you do for God, but Christianity is predicated on what God has done for man."[4]

ENDNOTES

Chapter 1

1. Mark Crawford, *The Obsessive-Compulsive Trap – Real Help for a Real Struggle* (Ventura, CA: Regal Books, 2004), 10.

Chapter 2

1. John Bunyan, *Grace Abounding to the Chief of Sinners* (Abbotsford, WI: Aneko Press, 2017), 127.
2. Jeff Wells, *Breaking Free of OCD: My Battle with Mental Pain and How God Rescued Me* (Houston, TX: Lucid Books, 2016), 5–6.

Chapter 3

1. Lee Strobel, *The Case for Faith – A Journalist Investigates the Toughest Objections to Christianity* (Grand Rapids, MI: Zondervan, 2000), 33–34.
2. "The Unmoved Rock," Bible.org, July 20, 2009, https://bible.org/illustration/unmoved-rock.
3. Hannah Whitall Smith, *The Christian's Secret of a Happy Life* (Grand Rapids, MI: Fleming H. Revell, 1952), 124–125.
4. "The Monet Analogy," Molecular Biometrics, https://web.archive.org/web/20080216221317/http://www.molecularbiometrics.com/monet_analogy.html.

Chapter 4

1. Charles Spurgeon, *Grace and Power: God's Free Favor, Your Spiritual Authority* (New Kensington, PA: Whitaker House, 2000), 217.
2. Spurgeon, *Grace and Power*, 275–276.
3. Spurgeon, 277.
4. James Strong, *A Concise Dictionary of the Words in the Greek Testament*, s.v. "Gr. #3341" (Nashville, TN: Abington Press, 1890), 47.

Chapter 5

1. Jeffrey M. Schwartz, with Beverly Beyette, *Brain Lock: A Four-Step Self-Treatment Method to Change You Brain Chemistry* (New York: HarperCollins Publishers, Inc, 1996), Back cover image.
2. Ian Osborn, *Can Christianity Cure Obsessive-Compulsive Disorder?: A Psychiatrist Explores the Role of Faith in Treatment* (Grand Rapids, MI: Brazos Press, 2008), 120.
3. Smith, *Secret of a Happy Life*, 124.
4. Bunyan, *Grace Abounding*, 127.
5. Bunyan, 130.
6. Bunyan, 130.
7. Bunyan, 130–131.
8. Bunyan, 130–131.
9. Bunyan, 133.
10. John Bunyan, *Grace Abounding to the Chief of Sinners*, The Project Gutenberg eBook, transcribed from the 1905 Religious Tract Society edition by David Price, February 19, 2013, paragraph 201, https://www.gutenberg.org/files/654/654-h/654-h.htm.
11. Bunyan, *Grace Abounding*, 134–135.
12. "Two Boats and a Helicopter," IWT Ministries, July 19, 2022, https://itwministries.org/two-boats-and-a-helicopter/.

13. Strong, s.v. "Gr. #769," 16.
14. Paul Meier, Todd Clements, Jean Luc Bertrand, and David Mandt Sr., *Blue Genes: Breaking Free from the Chemical Imbalances That Affect Your Moods, Your Mind, Your Life, and Your Loved Ones* (Carol Stream, IL: Tyndale House Publishers, 2005), 11–12.
15. Strong, s.v. "Gr. #4993," 70.

Chapter 6

1. Mark Crawford, *The Obsessive-Compulsive Trap: Real Help for a Real Struggle* (Ventura, CA: Regal Books, 2004), 124.
2. Crawford, *Obsessive-Compulsive Trap*, 124.
3. Crawford, 124.
4. Crawford, 124–125.
5. Crawford, 125.

Chapter 7

1. Schwartz with Beyette, *Brain Lock*, 10–12.
2. Smith, *Secret of a Happy Life*, 124.
3. Evans, Tony (@drtonyevans). 2022. "Forgiveness is not pretending like it didn't happen or it didn't hurt. That's lying. Forgiveness is the decision to release a debt regardless of how you feel." Twitter, April 29, 2022, 3:18 PM. https://twitter.com/drtonyevans/status/1520165549170438149?lang=en.
4. "Red," *The Shawshank Redemption*, directed by Frank Darabont (1994: Beverly Hills, CA: Castle Rock Entertainment).

Chapter 8

1. Smith, *Secret of a Happy Life*, 80–81.
2. Schwartz with Beyette, *Brain Lock*, 10–12.
3. Schwartz with Beyette, 5.

4. Jeffery M. Schwartz, "Biola University Center for Christian Thought: Contributions by Jeffrey M. Schwartz," 2013–2019, https://cct.biola.edu/people/jeffrey-m-schwartz/.
5. Bunyan, *Grace Abounding*, 150–151.
6. Strong, s.v. "Gr. #26," 7.
7. Strong, s.v. "Gr. #5479," 77.
8. Strong, s.v. "Gr. #1515," 25.
9. Strong, s.v. "Gr. #3115," 46.
10. Strong, s.v. "Gr. 5544," 78.)
11. Strong, s.v. "Gr. #19," 7.
12. Strong, s.v. "Gr. #4102," 58.
13. Strong, s.v. "Gr. 1466," 25.
14. Strong, s.v. "Gr. 54," 7.
15. *Merriam-Webster*, s.v. "pureness," https://www.merriam-webster.com/dictionary/pureness.
16. Strong, s.v. "Gr. 1516," 25.
17. *Merriam-Webster*, s.v. "salutary," https://www.merriam-webster.com/dictionary/salutary.
18. *Merriam-Webster*, s.v. "peaceable," https://www.merriam-webster.com/dictionary/peaceable.
19. Strong, s.v. "Gr. 1933," 31.
20. Strong, s.v. "Gr. 2138," 33.
21. Strong, s.v. "Gr. 1656," 27.
22. Strong, s.v. "Gr. 87," 8.
23. Strong, s.v. "Gr. 505," 13.
24. Dictionary.com; https://www.dictionary.com/browse/dissimulate.
25. John F. Walvoord and Roy B. Zuck eds., *The Bible Knowledge Commentary: New Testament* (Colorado Springs, CO: David C. Cook, 2004), 601.

Chapter 9

1. Tony Evans, *The Grace of God* (Chicago, IL: Moody Publishers, 2004), 9.
2. Evans, *Grace of God*, 12.
3. Evans, *Grace of God*, 16.
4. Tony Evans, sermon entitled "The Concept of Grace," CD 1 of 12 in the series, "The Magnificent Grace of God," released in 2018. (Modifications made to phrasing used to make spoken work more appropriate for text form. Substance and spirit of what was spoken remains unchanged). Paraphrase of this sermon can also be found at https://sermons.love/tony-evans/3704-tony-evans-the-concept-of-grace.html.
5. Evans, "Concept of Grace," minute 2.
6. Evans, "Concept of Grace," minutes 6–7.
7. Evans, "Concept of Grace," minute 7.
8. Evans, "Concept of Grace," minute 5.
9. Evans, "Concept of Grace," minute 3.
10. Evans, "Concept of Grace," minute 18.
11. Evans, "Concept of Grace," minutes 29–31.
12. Osborn, *Can Christianity Cure Obsessive-Compulsive Disorder?*, 180.
13. Schwartz, *Brain Lock*, 96.

Appendix

1. Steve King, Sermon preached in the 2000s. Various versions of this story can also be found online.
2. Lee Strobel, *The Case for Christ* (Grand Rapids, MI: Zondervan, 1998).
3. Lee Strobel, *The Case for the Resurrection* (Grand Rapids, MI: Zondervan, 2009).
4. Evans, Sermon entitled "Concept of Grace."

ABOUT THE AUTHOR

Mike began struggling with OCD as a young child and has spent most of his life battling the disorder. By seeking God's wisdom through his own study of the Scripture and through the careful mentorship of his grandfather, a pastor theologian, Mike has identified many powerful tools for battling OCD that every Christian OCD sufferer should know. Mike uses this Biblical wisdom to evaluate common medical and psychological treatments for OCD, showing that viewing the disorder though the lense of Scripture can multiply the effectiveness of these treatments for those who believe.

Mike earned a BS in Mechanical Engineering with a minor in mathematics from Virginia Tech, followed by an MS in finance from George Washington University. Mike and his wife Rashel married in 2007 and moved from Virginia back to her home state of California in 2010 where they currently live with their daughter. Mike's favorite hobbies include sports photography and underwater photography.